Creat ... ets

S ... t

Publisher's Note: Raw or semi-cooked eggs should not be consumed by babies, toddlers, pregnant or breastfeeding women, the elderly or those suffering from a chronic illness.

Publisher & Creative Director: Nick Wells
Senior Project Editor: Catherine Taylor
Art Director: Mike Spender
Layout Design: Jane Ashley
Digital Design & Production: Chris Herbert

Special thanks to Ann Nicol, Robert Zakes, Esme Chapman and Frances Bodiam.

For all cake decorating supplies, colours and shimmers by mail order: **Squires Kitchen**, Squires Group, Squires House, 3 Waverley Lane, Farnham, Surrey, GU9 8BB. Tel: 0845 617 1801 www.squires-shop.com

Discover 1000s more inspiring baking and decorating ideas at **lakeland.co.uk**. For cookie cutters, sugarcraft supplies and bakeware by mail order: Lakeland, Alexandria Buildings, Windermere, Cumbria, LA23 1BQ. Tel: 01539 488 100.

This is a **FLAME TREE** Book

FLAME TREE PUBLISHING
Crabtree Hall, Crabtree Lane
Fulham, London SW6 6TY
United Kingdom
www.flametreepublishing.com

First published 2014

ISBN: 978-1-78361-119-5

Printed in Singapore

All images are courtesy of Flame Tree Publishing Limited except the following: courtesy of **Shutterstock.com** and © the following contributors: 10, 13b Gayvoronskaya_Yana; 11t Mark Herreid; 11b Tharakorn Arunothai; 12 Sea Wave; 13t mady70; 14b, 23t M. Unal Ozmen; 14t Svetlana Lukienko; 16b n7atal7i; 16t PLen; 17t bonchan; 17b Quanthem; 18t 6493866629; 18b Africa Studio; 20b PeterVrabel; 20t, Roxana Bashyrova; 21b ffolas; 21t Pamela Uyttendaele; 22 Sean van Tonder; 23b Planner; 25t Joerg Beuge; 45& 129, 47 & 95, 53 & 107, 65 & 149, 83, 89, 91, 113, 119, 121, 123, 135, 137, 157, 161, 163, 165, 167, 211, 215, 225, 227, 235 Ruth Black; 49& 193 Stakhov Yuriy; 51 Gyorgy Barna; 57& 205 MrGarry; 69t & 183, 69b & 187, 103, 125, 229 Dulce Rubia; 73b & 203 tratong; 74t Elena Elisseeva; 85, 99, 105, 117, 147, 171 Prezoom.nl; 87, 93, 133, 201, 239 Olga Lyubkina; 97 Rockvilepikephotographs; 101, 111, 151, 177 Elisabeth Coelfen; 115 Mariya Volik; 127 Elena Schweitzer; 131 Olga_Phoenix; 139, 223, 233 John Kroetch; 141 longtaildog; 143, 189 Ksju; 145 Szasz-Fabian Jozsef; 159, 231 Karen H. Ilagan; 175 nick vangopoulos; 179 Gordana Sermek; 181 Chamille White; 185 stockcreations; 191 Undivided; 195 Irina Kupenska; 197 Danny E Hooks; 199 Paul Rich Studio; 209 Pete Pahham; 217 Artazum; 219 Portokalis; 221, 241 Christina Richards; 237 Koraysa; 243 Daniele Pietrobelli; courtesy of **iStockphoto**: 169 dwservingHim; 173 Kieren-Weich; 213 Ricardo-Toledo; courtesy of **LAKELAND**: 19b, 37, 60t, 61t, 62t, 62c, 63b.

Creative and Practical Projects

Sugarcraft

**FLAME TREE
PUBLISHING**

Contents

Introduction

Sugarcraft is a fun, satisfying and rewarding hobby. This book will give you lots of new ideas and sets out to help you make your cakes and cookies look really special. Each project is illustrated with beautiful photographs of the finished design to inspire you to create attractive and impressive cakes and cookies. The front section tells you everything you will need to know about basic recipes and equipment, how to master covering techniques, as well as piping and making decorations for a professional finish.

Iced cookies have become so popular and there are lots of pretty cookie cutters on sale in all shapes and sizes. If you don't have special cutters, you'll find templates and stencils included at the back of the book to help you. Icing and making decorations takes time and patience and it is important, especially before starting a complicated design, to read right through the instructions carefully and allow yourself plenty of time to complete all the stages. If a project looks difficult, you can make some pieces, such as models or flowers, up to a month ahead and then reduce the last-minute work involved in making the whole item.

This book is split into four sections: Seasonal Sugarcraft includes projects for special times of the year such as Easter, Halloween and Christmas; Tea Party Pretty covers those lovely cakes and cookies you will be proud to serve for morning coffee, afternoon tea or a special birthday party; Celebrations & Special Occasions has some stunning goodies for for more formal occasions such as baby showers, christenings, weddings, engagements and birthday parties; while the last section covers Children's & Novelty – these enchanting cakes and cookies are ideal for parties, with old favourites like teddy bears and colourful new cakes for both boys and girls and the young at heart.

These delightful projects show a variety of styles and techniques, but you can have fun adapting them yourself and creating your own unique designs. So be inspired and enjoy your hobby, making something special for everyone.

Ann Nicol

Baking
Basics

Beautiful sugarcraft decorations really put the cherry on top of a delicious homemade cake. Before you get stuck in to learning the intricacies of this fantastic craft, take a moment to brush up on your baking basics so your finished cakes not only look great, but taste amazing too! This section covers all the ingredients, key equipment, basic techniques and basic recipes you will need to bake everything from a classic fruit cake to vanilla cupcakes, cake pops and gingerbread ready for decorating.

Ingredients

In baking, most cakes are made by mixing sugar, fats, flour and eggs together. During the mixing, air is incorporated into the mixture to greater or lesser degrees to make it rise during baking. As a cake mixture bakes, the strands of gluten in the flour are stretched and the heat hardens them to give a light sponge-like texture.

Sugar

Sugar is not just included to give sweetness to cakes, it also produces a structure and texture that make a cake tender, so always choose the correct type for your recipe.

∾ Granulated Sugar – This is the standard sugar that you add to your tea. It comes in white and golden unrefined varieties and is used for toppings. The coarseness of granulated sugar means that it does not dissolve easily and is not designed for most baking recipes, so is no good for the creaming method.

∾ Caster Sugar – This is a fine-ground granulated sugar, which also comes in white and golden (or 'natural') unrefined varieties. It blends easily with butter and margarine when beaten or 'creamed' into light sponge mixtures.

∾ Soft Light and Dark Brown Sugars – These cream well and are usually used in richer cakes or spicy fruit mixtures such as carrot cake, and in recipes where rich colour and flavour are needed. Store this sugar in a tightly sealed container to prevent it from drying out. If it does become dry or lumpy, pound it back into crystals with the flat end of a rolling pin before you use it.

- **Muscovado Sugar** – This sugar is natural and unrefined, with a deep brown colour and rich flavour that makes fruit cakes extra special. It comes in light and dark varieties.

Eggs

- **Storing** – Always store eggs in the refrigerator, but remove them an hour or so before you start to bake, as better results will be achieved if you allow them to reach room temperature before using. This is because, at this temperature, eggs will whisk better and achieve more aeration.

  This not only gives more volume to the mixture, but also allows the eggs to blend in more easily. Cold eggs used straight from the refrigerator can curdle or split a mixture.

- **Egg Types** – Eggs sold as 'value' or 'economy' can be used for baking cakes and cupcakes, particularly if you are working to a budget (but do not forget the welfare issues involved in this choice). Also, do remember that these may be ungraded and of different sizes, so, for best results, buy eggs marked as 'medium' and 'large'. If you do use economy eggs, make sure to note the sizes you are using and try to even out the quantity by, say, using one large and two small eggs instead of three medium-sized ones.

Ingredients

Egg Powder – Dried egg-white powder gives good results and can be substituted in royal icing recipes, or in recipes where you are unsure about using raw egg whites in the case of pregnant women, the very young or the elderly.

Flours

Plain white flour provides the structure of a cake or biscuit, but contains nothing to make it rise, so cakes and cookies that do not need raising agents are made with plain flour. Most recipes using plain flour have bicarbonate of soda or baking powder added to them to make the cakes rise. It is always advisable to sift this into the mixture to incorporate the raising agents evenly.

Self-raising Flour – This has raising agents already added, that will add air to make a cake rise, so is used for light sponge mixtures. If you have only plain flour available, add 2^1/$_2$ tsp baking powder to 225 g/ 8 oz plain flour to make it into a self-raising flour.

Storing Flour – White flours should be stored in a cool dry place for up to six months, but wholemeal flours will not keep as long, as they have a higher fat content, so check the use-by date on all packs. Flour is best stored in a sealed airtight container. Always wash and dry this thoroughly before refilling and never add new flour to old. Small micro-organisms will form in very old flour, from the protein, and these can be seen as tiny black specks that will spread into new flour. If you do not have a container, store the opened paper bag inside a large plastic bag and make sure all flour is kept dry. Damp flour weighs more and therefore alters the recipe, which could lead to heavy or flat cakes.

Raising Agents

Raising agents are added to flour to make cakes rise and produce a light texture. It is important to be accurate when measuring these fine powders out, so always use a measuring spoon.

- ❧ Baking Powder – This is a mixture of bicarbonate of soda and cream of tartar. When liquid is added, the powder fizzes and bubbles and produces carbon dioxide, which expands with heat during baking and gives an airy texture. Be careful not to use very hot or boiling liquid in mixtures, as these can reduce the power of baking powder.

- ❧ Bicarbonate of Soda or Baking Soda – This is a gentler raising agent and is often used to give melted or spicy mixtures a lift. Cakes will have a bitter flavour if too much is added, so measure this out carefully and accurately with a proper measuring spoon, not a domestic teaspoon.

Fats

Fat adds structure, texture and flavour to cakes and improves their keeping qualities. Always remove them from the refrigerator before using them – they are much easier to mix in when at room temperature.

- ❧ Butter and Hard Block Margarine – Butter and hard margarine can be interchanged in a recipe, and the results will be the same. Butter, however, will always

❧   Ingredients

give a better flavour to cakes and cookies, so, if they are for a special occasion, is it well worth spending a little extra on this.

> ∾ Soft Margarine – Sold in tubs, this is wonderful for using in all-in-one sponge recipes where all the ingredients are quickly mixed together in one bowl. This fat always produces good results and is quick and easy to use because it does not have to be used at room temperature but can be taken straight from the refrigerator. Do not substitute soft margarine for butter or hard block margarine in a recipe, as it is a totally different kind of fat, which will not produce the same results.

Cakes using soft margarine usually require extra raising agent, so do follow the recipe carefully and do not be tempted to over-beat the mixture, as it will become wet and the cakes may sink. Up to 2 minutes of whisking with an electric mixer is fine to make a smooth mixture.

Dried Fruits

> ∾ Dried Vine Fruits – Fruits such as raisins, currants, sultanas and cranberries are usually sold ready-washed and prepared for baking, but it is still worth looking through them for pieces of stalk and grit before baking. Dried cranberries, sometimes sold as 'craisins', add a sweet, fresh flavour to cakes, similar to dried cherries. As they are bright red in colour, these can be used as a topping or decoration, as well as baked into mixtures. Fresh cranberries also make a colourful cake decoration.

> ∾ Glacé Cherries – Sold thinly coated in syrup, these come in a dark maroon natural colour and a brighter red colour, the latter usually being cheaper than the natural variety. These cherries keep well stored in their tubs in a cool place. Always wash the syrup off the cherries before baking, as it will cause the cherries to sink in the mixture.

- **Citrus Peels** – Bright and colourful, these add a zesty tang to recipes. Dried orange, lemon and lime peels can be bought as whole large pieces in syrup or a sugar glaze, or ready chopped into small pieces coated in light syrup in a tub (often sold as 'mixed peel'). Keep both varieties in a cool place to prevent crystallisation or drying out of the fruit.

- **Dried Apricots** – Dried apricots are a great addition to fruit cakes and are richer and sweeter than the fresh fruits. Some dried apricots are shrivelled and have a dark brown colour and these need soaking before use. Look for packs of the ready-to-eat varieties, which are soft and moist and ready to use for baking. Organic dried apricots usually have a brighter orange colour and a better flavour, so are worth looking out for.

Spices

Most dried spices have a reasonably long shelf life but will not keep indefinitely, and remember that they will gradually lose their aroma and flavour. It is a good idea to buy in small quantities only when you need them. You will find that both light and heat affect the power and flavour of spices, so, if stored in clear glass jars, keep them out of the light – the best place to store spices is in a dark, cool, dry place.

Flavourings

Flavouring extracts are very concentrated and usually sold in liquid form in small bottles. For example, a teaspoon measure will usually be enough to flavour a cake mixture for 12 cupcakes.

Ingredients

Vanilla and almond extracts are ideal to impart their delicate flavours into cake mixtures and you will find the more expensive extracts give a finer and more natural flavour. Rosewater can be used for flavouring both cake mixtures and icings and has a delicate, perfumed flavour. Fruit flavourings, such as lemon, lime, orange and raspberry, will give a fresh twist to mixtures and icings.

Chocolate

Indulgent chocolate is a useful ingredient for any cake decorator, whether used just to make the cake itself or as a delicious icing too. For the best results and a professional finish and flavour, it is always advisable to buy the highest-quality chocolate you can find, although this will be more expensive. Better-quality chocolates contain a higher percentage of real cocoa fat, which gives a flavour and texture far superior to cheaper varieties.

Cheaper chocolate labelled as 'cooking' or 'baking' chocolate contains a much lower percentage of cocoa solids and is best avoided in favour of better-quality eating chocolate.

The amount of cocoa fat or solids contained in chocolate will be marked on the wrapper of any good-quality chocolate. Those marked as 70 per cent (or more) cocoa solids will give the best results and you will find that this chocolate is shiny and brittle and it should snap very easily.

Dark Chocolate – Also known as 'plain' or 'plain dark' chocolate, this is the most useful all-purpose type of chocolate for baking, as it has a good strong flavour.

Milk Chocolate – Milk chocolate has sugar added and is sweeter than dark, so is also good for melting for icings and decorations.

White Chocolate – This is not strictly chocolate, as it contains only cocoa butter, milk and sugar. It is expensive and the most difficult to work with, so must be used with care. It is best to grate it finely and keep the temperature very low when melting it.

Chocolate Cake Covering – This is a cheaper substitute, which contains a minimum of 2.5 per cent cocoa solids and vegetable oil. It is considerably cheaper than real chocolate and the flavour is not as good, but it is easy to melt and sets quickly and well for a coating.

Cocoa Powder – Cocoa powder needs to be cooked to release the full flavour, so blend it with boiling water to make into a paste, then cool, before adding to a recipe, or sift it into the bowl with the flour.

Drinking Chocolate – Be aware that this is not the same as cocoa, as it contains milk powder and sugar. Some recipes may specify using drinking chocolate and these are successful, but do not substitute it for cocoa powder, as it will spoil the flavour of a cake.

Ingredients

Key Equipment

Bakeware

It is worth investing in a selection of high-quality tins and trays, which, if looked after properly, should last for many years. Choose heavy-duty metalware that will not buckle or the new flexible silicone trays – these are easy to turn out, most need very little greasing and they also wash and dry easily.

↪ Deep Cake Tins – With deep cake tins, you can buy both round or square (or even shaped) tins, depending on preference. They vary in size from 12.5–35.5 cm/5–14 inches with a depth of between 12.5–15 cm/5–6 inches. A deep cake tin for everyday fruit or Madeira cake is a must; a useful size is 20 cm/8 inches.

↪ Metal Muffin Trays – Muffin trays come in different weights and sizes; they are generally available with six or 12 deep-set holes. When purchasing, buy the heaviest type you can – although these will be expensive, they produce the best results, as they have good heat distribution and do not buckle. Muffin trays can vary in the size and depth of hole, which obviously affects the eventual size of the muffin.

If using trays without a nonstick finish, it is advisable to give these a light greasing before use. To grease trays, apply a thin film of melted vegetable margarine with a pastry brush or rub round the tray with kitchen paper and a little softened butter or margarine. You will normally need to line metal muffin trays with deep paper muffin cases or strips of baking parchment.

Silicone Muffin Trays and Cupcake Cases – These are flexible and produce very good results. Although they are sold as nonstick, it is still advisable to rub round each hole or case with a little oil on kitchen paper to prevent sticking. Silicone cupcake cases come in many bright colours and, unlike paper cases, are reusable. Simply wash out any crumbs after use in soapy water and leave them to dry, or clean them in the dishwasher.

Paper Cupcake Cases – These come in many varieties, colours and shapes. It is advisable to buy the more expensive types, which are thicker and give a good shape to the cake as it rises. Oil and moisture is less likely to penetrate the thicker cases, whereas it may show through the cheaper ones. Metallic gold, silver and coloured cupcake cases give good results and create a stunning effect for a special occasion. Cupcake cases also come in mini-muffin sizes. These may not be so easy to find, but can be bought from mail-order cake decoration suppliers.

Cake Pop Baking Moulds – These are silicone or metal tins that come in two halves and have 12 small round indentations for the cake mix. Fill one half of the tin and clamp the other tin on top and, as the mixture rises, it will form perfect spheres. The round cakes are placed on thin lollipop sticks before decorating.

Mini Cake Tins and Moulds – These are small square or round domed cake tins that measure approximately 5 cm/2 inches across and make small individual cakes. You can buy mini cake pans with detachable grids that will make both square and round shapes.

Baking Sheets and Trays – When baking cookies or biscuits, perhaps the most important piece of equipment is the sheet or tray that they are baked on. A nonstick baking sheet

Key Equipment

as opposed to a tray is preferable. This is because, without the higher sides of a tray, the heat penetrates the uncooked dough more quickly, giving a more uniform colour and texture. If the sheet is lightly oiled, then the cooked cookies or biscuits, with the aid of a palette knife, can be gently lifted onto a wire cooling rack without fear of them breaking.

Baking Papers and Foil – Nonstick baking 'parchment' or 'paper' is useful for lining the bases of small tins or for drying out chocolate and sugarpaste shapes.

Greaseproof paper is needed for making triangular paper icing bags. Baking parchment can be used, but greaseproof paper is better, as it is thinner and more flexible.

A large sheet of kitchen foil is handy for wrapping cakes or for protecting wrapped cakes in the freezer.

Useful Items

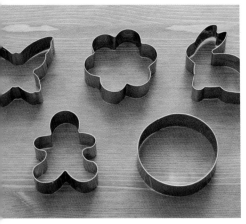

Mixing Bowls – Three to four different sizes of mixing bowls are very useful for mixing and melting ingredients.

Cutters – Cookie cutters for almost any imaginable shape can be bought from specialist cake and baking stores. They come in classic metal styles, in plastic, or as plunger-style.

- **Measuring Items** – Baking needs 100 per cent accuracy to ensure a perfect result. Scales come in many shapes and sizes, both digital and with weights. Most have a weigh pan, although, with some, your own bowl is used. Measuring jugs and spoons are essential for accurate measuring of both your dry and wet ingredients.

- **Mixing Spoons and Sieves** – Basic mixing cutlery is also essential, such as a wooden spoon (for mixing and creaming), a spatula (for transferring the mixture from the mixing bowl to the baking tins and spreading the mixture once it is in the tins) and a palette knife (to ease cakes out of their tins before placing them on the wire racks to cool). Also, do not forget a fine-mesh sieve for sifting flour and powders.

- **Cake Tester or Skewer** – Use a small, thin metal skewer for inserting into the centre of a cake to test if the cake is ready. This is a handy piece of equipment but, if you do not have one, a clean, thin metal knitting needle may be used instead.

- **Wire Cooling Racks** – Another vital piece of equipment is a wire cooling rack. It is essential when baking to allow cakes and biscuits to cool after being removed from their tins.

  A wire rack also protects your kitchen surfaces from the heat and allows air to circulate around the goodies, speeding cooling and preventing soggy bottoms.

- **Pastry Brush** – A pastry brush is used for brushing glazes over cakes and melted butter round tins. As brushes tend to wear out regularly and shed their bristles, keep a spare new brush to hand.

- **Palette Knives** – A small and a large palette knife are ideal for many jobs, including loosening cakes from their tins, lifting cakes

Key Equipment

and biscuits and swirling on buttercream frosting. A palette knife with a cranked blade is useful for lifting small cakes or flat pieces of sugarpaste.

⤸ Kitchen Scissors – Scissors are essential for many small jobs, including cutting papers to size and snipping cherries, dried fruits or nuts into chunks.

⤸ Grater – A grater is useful for grating citrus zests, chocolate and marzipan or almond paste. Choose one with a fine and a coarse side.

Electrical Equipment

Nowadays, help from time-saving gadgets and electrical equipment makes baking far easier and quicker. There is a wide choice of machines available, from the most basic to the highly sophisticated.

⤸ Food Processors – When choosing a machine, decide first what you need your processor to do. If you are a novice, it may be a waste to start with a machine which offers a wide range of implements and functions. This can be off-putting and result in not using the machine to its ultimate potential. When buying a food processor, look for measurements on the sides of the processor bowl and machines with a removable feed tube, which allows food or liquid to be added while the motor is still running. Look out for machines that have the facility to increase the capacity of the bowl and have a pulse button for controlled chopping. For many, storage is an issue, so reversible discs and flex storage, or, on more advanced models, a blade storage compartment or box, can be advantageous.

It is also worth thinking about machines which offer optional extras which can be bought as your cooking requirements change. Mini chopping bowls are available for those wanting to chop small quantities of food. If time is an issue, dishwasher-friendly attachments may be vital. Citrus presses, liquidisers and whisks may all be useful attachments for the individual cook.

Table-top Mixers – Table-top mixers are freestanding and are capable of dealing with fairly large quantities of mixture. They are robust machines and good for heavy cake mixing as well as whipping cream, whisking egg whites or making one-stage cakes. They also offer a wide range of attachments, ranging from liquidisers to mincers, juicers, can openers and many more and varied attachments.

Hand-held Mixers – A hand-held electric mixer makes quick work of whisking butter and sugar and is an invaluable aid for cake baking. They are smaller than freestanding mixers and often come with their own bowl and stand from which they can be lifted off and used as hand-held devices. They have a motorised head with detachable twin whisks.

These mixers are versatile, as they do not need a specific bowl in which to whisk. Any suitable mixing bowl can be used. Do not be tempted to use a food processor for mixing small amounts, as it is easy to over-process and this may produce flat cakes.

Key Equipment

Basic Cake-making Techniques

Lining Cake Tins

If a recipe states that the tin needs lining, do not be tempted to ignore this. Rich fruit cakes and other cakes that take a long time to cook benefit from the tin being lined so that the edges and base do not burn or dry out. Greaseproof paper or baking parchment is ideal for this. It is a good idea to have the paper at least double thickness, or preferably three or four thicknesses. Sponge cakes and other cakes that are cooked in 30 minutes or less are also better if the bases are lined, as it is far easier to remove them from the tin.

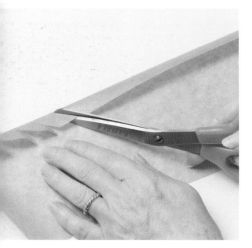

The best way to line a round or square tin is to lightly draw around the base and then cut just inside the markings, making it easy to sit in the tin. Next, lightly grease the paper so that it will easily peel away from the cake.

If the sides of the tin also need to be lined, then cut a strip of paper long enough for the tin. This can be measured by wrapping a piece of string around the rim of the tin. Once again, lightly grease the paper, push against the tin and oil once more, as this will hold the paper to the sides of the tin.

Separating Eggs

When separating eggs (that is, separating the white from the yolk), crack an egg in half lightly and cleanly over a bowl, being careful not to break the yolk and keeping it in the shell. Then tip the yolk backwards and forwards between the two shell halves, allowing as much of the white as possible to spill out into the bowl. Keep or discard the yolk and/or the white as needed. Make sure that you do not get any yolk in your whites, as this will prevent successful whisking of the whites. It takes practice!

Making Methods

∿ **Creaming** – Light cakes, and biscuits, are made by the creaming method, which means that the butter and sugar are first beaten or 'creamed' together. A little care is needed for this method. Using a large mixing bowl, beat the fat and sugar together until pale and fluffy. The eggs are gradually beaten in to form a slackened batter and the flour is folded in last, to stiffen up the mixture. In some recipes, egg whites are whisked and added to the mixture separately for extra lightness.

When the eggs are added, they are best used at room temperature to prevent the mixture from splitting or 'curdling'. Adding a teaspoon of flour with each beaten egg will help to keep the mixture light and smooth and prevent the mixture from separating. A badly mixed, curdled batter will hold less air and be heavy or can cause a sunken cake.

∿ **All-in-one Mixtures** – This 'one stage' method is quick and easy and is perfect for those new to baking, as it does not involve any complicated techniques. It is ideal for making light sponges, but soft tub-type margarine or softened butter at room temperature must be used. There is no need for any creaming or rubbing in, as all the ingredients are simply placed in a large bowl and quickly beaten together for just a few minutes until smooth. Be careful not to over-beat, as this will make the mixture too wet. Self-raising flour with the addition of a little extra baking powder is vital for a good rise.

⌒ Fruit Cakes – Rich fruit cakes are usually made by the creaming method, then dried fruits and nuts are folded into the mixture last.

Checking to See if the Bakes are Cooked

For light sponge-type cakes, press the centre lightly with the fingertips and, if the cake is cooked, it should spring back easily. To test more thoroughly, insert a thin, warmed skewer into the deepest part of the centre. If the cake is cooked, it will come out perfectly clean with no mixture sticking to it, but, if there is some mixture on the skewer, bake the cake for a little longer and test again.

Small cupcakes should be golden, risen and firm to the touch when pressed lightly in the centre. The last part of a cupcake to cook is the centre, so, after the baking time stated, check this area.

Biscuits are cooked when they are just starting to turn an even golden colour. Remove the trays from the oven and transfer each whole sheet of baking paper to a cooling rack or lift each biscuit away with a palette knife, but do this carefully as they are fragile when hot.

How to Patch Up Mistakes

If the cakes are overcooked or are burnt on the outside, simply scrape this away with a serrated knife and cover the surface with buttercream. If the cakes are a little dry, sprinkle them with a few drops of sweet sherry or orange juice.

Cutting the Tops Level

Many cakes and cupcakes form a small peak while baking. However, some methods of decorating cakes require a flat surface, so, for these, trim the tops level with a knife. You can also coat cupcakes with apricot glaze and press on a disc of almond paste or sugarpaste to give a flat surface to decorate (*see* pages 42 and 48).

Storing Cakes and Biscuits

Chocolate and Madeira cakes can be made ahead of time and will store well for up to 5 days before decorating. Cover in fresh baking parchment, then wrap in foil and keep in a cool place, or, alternatively, freeze for up to 2 months.

Rich fruit cakes should be stored before cutting and need at least 1 month for the flavour to mature. Wedding cakes should be made 3 months ahead to give them a better flavour and enable the cake to become moist enough to cut cleanly into slices. Wrap rich fruit cakes in their baking papers, then overwrap in clean baking parchment, then a double layer of foil and seal with tape. Keep the cakes in a cool place until required.

Biscuits are best stored in an airtight cake tin lined with waxed paper or kitchen foil. Layer them with further sheets of waxed paper or kitchen foil. Use a tin rather than a plastic lidded container, as the latter keep moisture in and will make cookies go soggy. Store different types of cookie separately and preferably un-iced.

Basic Recipes

Rich Fruit Cake

Square Cake Size	13 cm/5 inch square	16 cm/6 inch square	18 cm/7 inch square
Round Cake Size	15 cm/6 inch round	18 cm/7 inch round	20 cm/8 inch round
sultanas	125 g/4 oz	175 g/6 oz	225 g/8 oz
raisins	125 g/4 oz	175 g/6 oz	225 g/8 oz
currants	125 g/4 oz	175 g/6 oz	225 g/8 oz
chopped mixed peel	50 g/2 oz	75 g/3 oz	125 g/4 oz
glacé cherries, chopped	50 g/2 oz	75 g/3 oz	125 g/4 oz
lemons	$^1/_2$	$^1/_2$	1
dark rum or fresh orange juice	2 tbsp	3 tbsp	4 tbsp
butter, softened	125 g/4 oz	175 g/6 oz	225 g/8 oz
soft dark muscovado sugar	125 g/4 oz	175 g/6 oz	225 g/8 oz
plain flour	125 g/4 oz	175 g/6 oz	225 g/8 oz
mixed spice	$^1/_2$ tsp	1 tsp	2 tsp
ground almonds	25 g/1 oz	50 g/2 oz	75 g/3 oz
eggs, beaten	2	3	4–5
dark treacle	2 tsp	1 tbsp	1 tbsp
Cooking time 1	30 mins	50 mins	1 hour
Cooking time 2	1 hour 30 mins	1 hour 40 mins	$2^1/_4$ hours

Square Cake Size	20 cm/8 inch square	23 cm/9 inch square	25 cm/10 inch square
Round Cake Size	23 cm/9 inch round	25 cm/10 inch round	28 cm/11 inch round
sultanas	275 g/10 oz	350 g/12 oz	450 g/1 lb
raisins	275 g/10 oz	350 g/12 oz	450 g/1 lb
currants	275 g/10 oz	350 g/12 oz	450 g/1 lb
chopped mixed peel	150 g/5 oz	175 g/6 oz	200 g/7 oz
glace cherries, chopped	150 g/5 oz	175 g/6 oz	200 g/7 oz
lemons	1	$1^1/_2$	2
dark rum or fresh orange juice	2 tbsp	4 tbsp	6 tbsp
butter, softened	275 g/10 oz	350 g/12 oz	450 g/1 lb
soft dark muscovado sugar	275 g/10 oz	350 g/12 oz	450 g/1 lb
plain flour	275 g/10 oz	350 g/12 oz	450 g/1 lb
mixed spice	15 ml/1 tbsp	15 ml/1 tbsp	15 ml/1 tbsp
ground almonds	125 g/4 oz	125 g/4 oz	150 g/5 oz
eggs, beaten	5–6	6	8
dark treacle	1 tbsp	1 tbsp	2 tbsp
Cooking time 1	1 hour 30 mins	1 hour 50 mins	2 hours
Cooking time 2	$2^1/_2$–3 hours	3 hours	$3^1/_4$ hours

Basic Recipes

Before you start to bake, place the sultanas, raisins, currants, peel and cherries in a large bowl. Finely grate in the zest from the lemon and add the dark rum or freshly squeezed orange juice. Stir, cover and leave to soak overnight, or for 24 hours if possible.

Preheat the oven to 150°C/300°F/Gas Mark 2. Grease and line the tin with a triple layer of nonstick baking parchment.

Cream the butter and muscovado sugar in a large bowl until light and fluffy. Sift the flour and mixed spice together in a separate bowl, then stir in the ground almonds.

Add the eggs to the creamed mixture, a little at a time, adding a teaspoon of flour with each addition. Fold the remaining flour into the bowl, then add the treacle and soaked fruits. Stir well until the mixture is soft, smooth and well blended.

Spoon the mixture into the tin, then make a hollow in the centre of the mixture with the back of a large spoon.

Tie a layer of newspaper round the outside of the tin and bake according to cooking time 1, then reduce the heat to 120°C/250°F/Gas Mark 1/2 for cooking time 2.

If the top of the cake starts to brown too much, cover with a layer of damp, crumpled baking parchment. Test the cake by inserting a skewer into the centre; it should come out with no mixture sticking to it.

Cool the cake in the tin and then remove, leaving the lining papers on. Wrap the cake in an extra layer of baking parchment, then tightly in foil and leave to mature for 1–3 months in a cool place.

Rich Chocolate Cake

Square Cake Size	13 cm/5 inch square	18 cm/7 inch square	23 cm/9 inch square
Round Cake Size	15 cm/6 inch round	20 cm/8 inch round	25 cm/10 inch round
plain chocolate	50 g/2 oz	125 g/4 oz	225 g/8 oz
soft dark brown sugar	150 g/5 oz	275 g/10 oz	575g/1^1/$_4$lb 3oz
milk	135 ml/4^1/$_2$ fl oz	200 ml/7 fl oz	500 ml/18 fl oz
butter, softened	50 g/2 oz	125 g/4 oz	225 g/8 oz
eggs, beaten	1	3	6
plain flour	125 g/4 oz	225 g/8 oz	450 g/1 lb
bicarbonate of soda	^{1}/$_2$ tsp	1 tsp	2 tsp
Cooking time	45 mins	1 hour	1^1/$_2$ hours

Preheat the oven to 180°C/350°F/Gas Mark 4. Grease and line the tin with nonstick baking parchment. Break the chocolate into small pieces and place in a heavy-based pan with one third of the sugar and all of the milk. Heat gently until the chocolate has melted, then remove from the heat and cool.

Beat the butter and remaining sugar together until fluffy, then beat in the eggs a little at a time. Gradually beat in the cold melted chocolate mixture.

Sift the flour and bicarbonate of soda into the mixture and fold together with a large metal spoon until smooth. Bake for the time shown on the chart or until a skewer inserted into the centre comes out clean.

Cool for 10 minutes, then turn out of the tin onto a wire rack to cool. Store wrapped in foil until needed, or freeze wrapped tightly in foil for up to 3 months.

Madeira Cake

Square Cake Size	13 cm/5 inch square	16 cm/6 inch square	18 cm/7 inch square
Round Cake Size	15 cm/6 inch round	18 cm/7 inch round	20 cm/8 inch round
butter, softened	175 g/6 oz	225 g/8 oz	350 g/12 oz
caster sugar	175 g/6 oz	225 g/8 oz	350 g/12 oz
self-raising flour	175 g/6 oz	225 g/8 oz	350 g/12 oz
plain flour	75 g/3 oz	125 g/4 oz	175 g/6 oz
eggs	3	4	6
vanilla extract	$1/2$ tsp	1 tsp	1 tsp
glycerine	1 tsp	1 tsp	1 tsp
Cooking time	1 hour	$1-1^1/_4$ hours	$1^1/_4 - 1^1/_2$ hours

Square Cake Size	20 cm/8 inch square	23 cm/9 inch square
Round Cake Size	23 cm/9 inch round	25 cm/10 inch round
butter, softened	450 g/1 lb	500 g/1 lb 2 oz
caster sugar	450 g/1 lb	500 g/1 lb 2 oz
self-raising flour	450 g/1 lb	500 g/1 lb 2 oz
plain flour	225 g/8 oz	250 g/9 oz
eggs	8	9
vanilla extract	2 tsp	1 tbsp
glycerine	2 tsp	1 tbsp
Cooking time	$1^1/_2 - 1^3/_4$ hours	$1^1/_2 - 1^3/_4$ hours

Preheat the oven to 160°C/325°F/Gas Mark 3. Grease and line the tin with nonstick baking parchment.

Cream the butter and caster sugar together in a large bowl until light and fluffy. Sift the flours together. Whisk the eggs into the mixture one at a time, adding a teaspoon of flour with each addition to prevent the mixture from curdling.

Add the remaining flour, the vanilla extract and glycerine to the mixture and fold together with a large metal spoon until the mixture is smooth.

Spoon into the tin and bake for the time shown on the chart until firm and well risen and a skewer inserted into the centre comes out clean.

Leave to cool in the tin for 10 minutes, then turn out onto a wire rack to cool. Wrap in foil and store for up to 3 days before decorating. Freeze wrapped in foil for up to 2 months.

- Bowl Shaped – To cook the cake in a 2 litre/4 pint ovenproof bowl, grease the bowl well and use the amounts for the 13 cm/5 inch square cake, baking for 45 minutes–1 hour.

- Lemon Variation – To make the lemon variation of the Madeira cake, you can simply omit the vanilla extract and add the same amount of finely grated lemon zest.

- Almond Variation – To make the almond variation of the Madeira cake, you can simply omit the vanilla extract and add the same amount of almond extract.

Basic Recipes

Basic Vanilla Cupcakes

Makes 12–14

125 g/4 oz caster sugar
125 g/4 oz soft tub margarine
2 medium eggs
125 g/4 oz self-raising flour
½ tsp baking powder
½ tsp vanilla extract

Preheat the oven to 190°C/375°F/Gas Mark 5. Line a bun tray with paper cases.

Place all the cupcake ingredients in a large bowl and beat with an electric mixer for about 2 minutes until light and smooth. Fill the paper cases halfway up with the mixture. Bake for about 15 minutes until firm, risen and golden.

Remove to a wire rack to cool. Keeps for 2–3 days in an airtight container. Can be frozen for up to 2 months, but the paper cases will come away when thawed and these will need replacing.

- **Chocolate Variation** – Omit the caster sugar and use soft light brown sugar instead. Sift 25 g/1 oz cocoa powder in with the flour and baking powder. Omit the vanilla extract and add 2 tbsp milk instead. Mix and bake as above.

- **Cherry & Almond Variation** – Add 50 g/2 oz finely chopped washed glacé cherries. Omit the vanilla extract and use almond extract instead. Mix and bake as above.

Basic Butter-rich Cookies

Makes 20–24

125 g/4 oz unsalted butter, softened
125 g/4 oz caster sugar, plus extra for sprinkling (optional)
1 medium egg yolk
1 tsp vanilla extract
225 g/8 oz plain white flour

Preheat the oven to 180°C/350°F/Gas Mark 4. Cream the butter with the sugar until light and fluffy, then beat in the egg yolk and vanilla extract, then add the flour. Mix until the mixture comes together and forms a ball in the base of the mixing bowl.

Place the dough on a lightly floured surface or board and knead until smooth. Either shape into small rounds and flatten with your hand, or roll out to a thickness of 5 mm/¼ inch and cut into rounds or shapes.

Place on lightly buttered or oiled baking sheets, leaving room for expansion. Prick lightly with a fork and, if liked, sprinkle with a little caster sugar. Bake in the preheated oven for 15 minutes, or until pale golden.

Remove from the oven and leave to cool for 2–3 minutes before transferring to wire cooling racks. Leave until cold before storing in airtight containers.

Helpful Hint – If liked, shape the dough into a roll, wrap in baking paper and clingfilm and store in the refrigerator for 1 week. Remove the dough from the refrigerator 20–30 minutes before using, or you can freeze, tightly wrapped, for up to 3 months. To use, thaw at room temperature and roll out and bake as above.

Basic Recipes

Gingerbread House Dough

For the recipe on page 106

8 tbsp golden syrup
3 tbsp soft light brown sugar
75 g/3 oz butter
450 g/1 lb plain flour
1 tsp ground mixed spice
1 tbsp ground ginger
2 tsp bicarbonate of soda
2 egg yolks

Preheat the oven to 190°C/375°F/Gas Mark 5.

Draw and cut out templates (*see* page 244).

Place the syrup, sugar and butter in a saucepan and heat gently until melted. Sift the flour, spices and bicarbonate of soda into a bowl.

Cool the melted mixture slightly, then pour into the bowl with the egg yolks. Knead the warm mixture to a soft dough and, while still warm, roll out between two sheets of nonstick baking parchment. Lift the top paper away and cut round the card template.

Lift away excess dough from the paper, slide the whole sheet of paper and dough onto a baking sheet and bake for 8-10 minutes. Leave to cool flat on the paper.

Repeat with the remaining dough and trimmings.

Vanilla Cake Pops

Makes 24

125 g/4 oz soft-tub margarine or softened butter
125 g/4 oz caster sugar
125 g/4 oz self-raising flour
2 eggs
1 tsp milk
1 tsp vanilla extract

Preheat the oven to 180°C/350°F/Gas Mark 4. Brush a 12-hole
cake pop mould with melted butter. Place all the ingredients
in a bowl and beat together for 2 minutes until smooth.

Spoon 1 heaped teaspoon into each mould, but do not overfill, as the mixture expands.
Clamp on the lid and bake for 12 minutes. Test by inserting a wooden toothpick into the
hole in the moulds – it should come out clean. Turn out to cool on a wire rack, clean
and re-grease the tin and bake another 12 cake balls.

Unbaked Cake Pops

Makes roughly 12 medium or 16 small

350 g/12 oz leftover or bought Madeira cake
175 g/6 oz white or milk chocolate, melted

Chop the Madeira cake and crumble into fine crumbs in a bowl. Pour in the melted chocolate and
stir with your hands to a stiff mixture, then mould into small balls. Place on a tray and chill in the
refrigerator for 2 hours until firm. Place on thin lollipop sticks and decorate.

Basic Recipes

Sugarcraft
Basics

The possibilities when working with sugarcraft are endless, but, before you let your imagination run wild, it's time to get up to speed on the basics. This section begins by covering decorating ingredients and key icing recipes from cream cheese frosting to sugarpaste icing. You'll also learn how to cover cakes and produce tiered cakes, as well as the secrets to using sugarpaste and flower paste to style your cake decorating to suit every theme or occasion.

Decorating Ingredients

There are a multitude of ingredients you can use to decorate your bakes. Below, you will find reference to many of the icings, colourings and edible decorations you can buy, as well as, later, key icing recipes, which will show you how to whip up your own icings from scratch. The basic icing recipes will be referenced often throughout the main recipe chapters.

Icing Sugar – Icing sugar is fine and powdery. It is usually sold plain and white, but can also be bought as an unrefined golden (or 'natural') variety. Use it for delicate icings, frostings and decorations. Store this sugar in a dry place, as it can absorb moisture and this will make it go hard and lumpy. Always sift this sugar at least once, or preferably twice, before you use it, to remove any hard lumps that would prevent icing from achieving a smooth texture – lumpy icing is impossible to pipe out.

Fondant Icing Sugar – This is sold in plain and flavoured varieties and gives a beautiful glossy finish to cake toppings. Just add a little boiled water to the sugar, according to the packet instructions, to make a shiny icing that can be poured or drizzled over cake tops to give a very professional finish. Colour the plain white icing with a few spots of paste food colouring to achieve your desired result.

Flavoured fondant icing sugar is sold in strawberry, raspberry, orange, lemon and blackcurrant flavours and also has colouring added. These sugars are ideal if you want to make a large batch of cakes with different coloured and flavoured toppings. Flavoured fondant sugars can also be whisked with softened unsalted butter and cream cheese to make delicious frostings in just a few moments.

Royal Icing Sugar – Royal icing sets to a classic, firm Christmas-cake-style covering or can be made to a softer consistency to give a glossy finish to cookies. Sold in packs as plain white sugar, this is whisked with cold water to give an instant royal icing. It has dried egg white included in the mixture, so does not need the long beating that traditional royal icing recipes require. It is also ideal to use for those who cannot eat raw egg whites.

Tubes of Writing Icing – You can buy small tubes of ready-coloured royal icing or gel icing, usually in sets of black, red, yellow and blue, and these are ideal for small amounts of writing or for piping on dots or small decorations.

Food Colourings – You can buy food colourings in liquid, paste, gel and powder or dust forms in a great range of colours:

Paste food colourings are best for using with sugarpaste. These are sold in small tubs and are very concentrated, so should be added to the sugarpaste dot by dot on the end of a wooden cocktail stick. Knead the colouring in evenly, adding more until you get the colour you require.

Liquid and gel food colourings are ideal for adding to frostings. Add this cautiously drop by drop, beating the frosting well until you reach the colour you require.

Dusts, sprays and lustre colourings should be lightly brushed onto dry sugarpaste with a paintbrush to form a delicate sheen to decorations such as flowers. Liquid paint and spray-on metallic colourings add a glossy sheen effect to decorations.

Coloured sugars can be made by adding a few dots of paste colouring to granulated sugar with a toothpick. Coloured sugars add sparkle to the sides of cakes, cookies and cupcakes.

Bought Sugar Decorations and Sprinkles – A range of sprinkles can be bought in supermarkets or by mail order from specialist cake decorating companies, and these provide a wonderful way to make quick and easy cake toppings.

41   Decorating Ingredients

Apricot Glaze & Almond Paste

Makes 450 g/1 lb to cover 2 x 20 cm/8 inch round cakes, or 24 small cakes

For the Apricot Glaze:

450 g/1 lb apricot jam
3 tbsp water
1 tsp lemon juice

For the Almond Paste:

125 g/4 oz sifted icing sugar
125 g/4 oz caster sugar
225 g/8 oz ground almonds
1 medium egg
1 tsp lemon juice

For the Apricot Glaze, place the jam, water and juice in a heavy-based saucepan and heat gently, stirring, until soft and melted.

Boil rapidly for 1 minute, then press through a fine sieve with the back of a wooden spoon. Discard the pieces of fruit.

Use immediately for glazing or sticking on almond paste, or pour into a clean jar or plastic airtight container and store in the refrigerator for up to 3 months.

For the Almond Paste, stir the sugars and ground almonds together in a bowl. Whisk the egg and lemon juice together and mix into the dry ingredients.

Knead until the paste is smooth. Wrap tightly in clingfilm or foil to keep airtight and store in the refrigerator until needed. The paste can be made 2–3 days ahead of time, but, after that, it will start to dry out and become difficult to handle.

To use the paste, knead on a surface dusted with icing sugar. Brush the top of each cake with apricot glaze. Roll out the almond paste to a circle large enough to cover the cake or cut out discs large enough to cover the tops of the cupcakes. Press onto the cakes. For how to cover large cakes with almond paste see page 66.

Basic Buttercream Frosting

Covers a 20 cm/8 inch round cake or 12 small cakes

Ingredients

150 g/5 oz unsalted butter, softened at room temperature
225 g/8 oz icing sugar, sifted
2 tbsp hot milk or water
1 tsp vanilla extract
food colourings of choice

Beat the butter until light and fluffy, then beat in the sifted icing sugar and hot milk or water in two batches.

Add the vanilla extract and any colourings. Store chilled for up to 2 days in an airtight container.

Variations
Omit the vanilla extract and instead:

- Coffee – Blend 2 tsp coffee extract with the milk.

- Chocolate – Blend 2 tbsp cocoa powder to a paste with 2 tbsp boiling water and use instead of the hot milk or water.

- Lemon – Beat in 1 tbsp fresh lemon juice, sieved.

Cream Cheese Frosting

**Covers a 20 cm/8 inch
round cake
or 12 small cakes**

Ingredients

50 g/2 oz unsalted butter,
softened at room temperature
300 g/11 oz icing sugar, sifted
flavouring of choice
food colourings of choice
125 g/4 oz full-fat cream cheese

Beat the butter and icing sugar together until light and fluffy.

Add flavourings and colourings of choice and beat again.

Add the cream cheese and whisk until light and fluffy.

Do not over-beat, however, as the mixture can become runny.

Sugarpaste Icing
(a.k.a. Fondant for Rolling or Modelling)

Makes 350 g/12 oz to cover a
20 cm/8 inch round cake
or 12 small cakes, or use
for decorations

Ingredients

1 medium egg white
1 tbsp liquid glucose
350 g/12 oz icing sugar, sifted,
plus extra for dusting

Place the egg white and liquid glucose in a large mixing bowl and stir together, breaking up the egg white.

Add the icing sugar gradually, mixing in until the mixture binds together and forms a ball.

Turn the ball of icing out onto a clean surface dusted with icing sugar and knead for 5 minutes until soft but firm enough to roll out.

If the icing is too soft, knead in a little more icing sugar until the mixture is pliable.

To colour, knead in paste food colouring. Do not use liquid food colouring, as this is not suitable and will make the sugarpaste limp.

To use, roll out thinly on a clean surface dusted with icing sugar to a circle large enough to cover a cake or cut out discs large enough to cover the top of each cupcake.

Flower Paste

Ingredients

2 tsp powdered gelatine
2 tsp liquid glucose
2 tsp white vegetable fat
450 g/1 lb sifted icing sugar
1 tsp gum tragacanth powder
1 egg white

Flower, petal or 'gum' paste is used for making very thin, delicate flowers and decorations, which set hard so that they can be handled easily.

Flower paste will roll out much more thinly than sugarpaste and is worth using for wedding cakes, as it gives a realistic finish to flowers, and these can be made ahead of time and easily stored. It can be bought from cake decorating suppliers or by mail order in small, ready-made slabs in different colours or as a powder that can be reconstituted with a little cold water and made into a paste.

To make your own, follow the recipe and store the paste in the refrigerator, tightly wrapped in strong plastic until needed.

Place 1¹/₂ tsp cold water in a heatproof bowl. Sprinkle over the gelatine and add the liquid glucose and white fat. Place the bowl over a saucepan of hot water and heat until melted, stirring occasionally. Cool slightly.

Sift the icing sugar and gum tragacanth powder into a bowl, make a well in the centre and add the egg white and the cooled gelatine mixture. Mix together to make a soft paste.

Knead the paste on a surface dusted with icing sugar until smooth, then wrap in clingfilm to exclude all air. Leave for 2 hours, then break off small pieces and use to make fine flowers and petals.

Royal Icing

Makes 500 g/1 lb 2 oz to cover a 20 cm/8 inch round cake or 12 small cakes

Ingredients

2 medium egg whites
500 g/1 lb 2 oz icing sugar, sifted
2 tsp lemon juice

Put the egg whites in a large bowl and whisk lightly with a fork to break up the whites until foamy.

Sift in half the icing sugar with the lemon juice and beat well with an electric mixer for 4 minutes, or by hand with a wooden spoon for about 10 minutes, until smooth.

Gradually sift in the remaining icing sugar and beat again until thick, smooth and brilliant white and the icing forms soft peaks when flicked up with a spoon.

Keep the royal icing covered with a clean damp cloth until ready for use, or store in the refrigerator in an airtight plastic container until needed.

If making royal icing to use later, beat it again before use to remove any air bubbles that may have formed in the mixture.

Modelling Chocolate

Ingredients

125 g/4 oz plain, milk or
white chocolate
2 tbsp liquid glucose

Break the chocolate into small pieces and melt in a
heatproof bowl standing over a pan of very gently
simmering water.

Remove from the heat and beat in the liquid glucose until a
paste forms that comes away from the sides of the bowl.

Place the paste in a plastic bag and chill for 1 hour until
firm, or store for up to 2 weeks in a tightly sealed
plastic bag.

To use, break off pieces and knead until pliable. Modelling
chocolate is ideal for making thin ribbons and flowers.

Chocolate Covering Icing

To cover a 20 cm/8 inch round cake

Ingredients

175 g/6 oz dark chocolate
2 tbsp liquid glucose
1 medium egg white
500 g/1 lb 2 oz sifted icing sugar

Break up the chocolate into pieces and melt in a heatproof bowl standing over a bowl of very gently simmering water. Add the liquid glucose and stir until melted.

Remove from the heat and cool for 5 minutes, then whisk in the egg white and half the sugar until smooth. When the mixture becomes stiff, turn out onto a flat surface and knead in the remaining icing sugar.

Wrap tightly in clingfilm and keep in a cool place for up to 3 days. To use, break off pieces and knead until soft and warm. Use quickly, as, when the paste cools, it will start to harden more quickly than sugarpaste.

Glacé Icing

Covers a 20 cm/8 inch
round cake (top)
or 12 small cakes

Ingredients

225 g/8 oz icing sugar
few drops lemon juice, vanilla or
almond extract
2–3 tbsp boiling water
liquid or paste
food colouring (optional)

Sift the icing sugar into a bowl and add the chosen flavouring, then gradually stir in enough water to mix to the consistency of thick cream.

Beat with a wooden spoon until the icing is thick enough to coat the back of the spoon, and add a few drops of liquid or paste food colouring, if desired. Use immediately, as the icing will begin to form a skin as it starts to set.

Sugarcraft Equipment

Ι

If you are to produce the best results possible, sugarcraft and cake decorating require a fair few more pieces of equipment than standard baking!

∾ **Cake Boards** – Thin and thicker drum-style boards are needed to give the cakes a good base.

∾ **Dowels** – Cake dowels are small, short pieces of thin plastic or wood that are used to support tiers of cake. Four dowels are usually inserted into a cake base at equal distances, to support the next layer placed on top.

∾ **Turntable** – A heavy-based icing turntable helps you coat the sides of a cake easily.

∾ **Plastic Rolling Pins** – A long plastic rolling pin is needed for easy rolling out of sugarpaste. Wooden pins can be used for almond paste, but are not good for sugarpaste, which tends to stick to them. A small plastic rolling pin is useful for rolling out small quantities of flower paste.

∾ **Boards** – Large plastic boards are useful if you do not have a nonstick kitchen surface and small plastic boards are vital for rolling out small pieces of flower paste.

∾ **Brushes** – A selection of fine-tipped paintbrushes should be kept just for adding painted-on details and dusting lustre powders onto sugarpaste projects.

∾ **Wooden Toothpicks** – Toothpicks are used for colouring, rolling and fluting scraps of flower paste, and lifting delicate pieces of sugarpaste into position.

• Scissors – A separate small pair of sharp, pointed scissors is needed for cutting out templates, snipping into sugarpaste and shaping with the pointed ends.

• Smoothers – Smoothers are essential for achieving a smooth finish on a sugarpaste-covered cake. Holding one in each hand will give a perfect top and sides to a cake.

• Spirit Level – A spirit level is needed for tiered cakes such as wedding cakes, to check that the levels are even and correct.

• Garlic or Icing Press – A press is used to achieve long strands of sugarpaste, such as hair on models.

• Wooden Spoon Handles and Spaghetti – Use wooden spoon handles wrapped in clingfilm for shaping ribbons and bows. Use short pieces of spaghetti for shaping difficult small areas.

• Tweezers – A pair of tweezers is useful for positioning small, delicate items or making a rough pattern in sugarpaste.

• Pins – Glass-headed dressmakers' pins keep templates in place.

• Wires – 20- and 26-gauge sugarcraft wires can be used for securing the stems and stalks of flowers.

• Floristry Tape – This tape is used to cover bunches of wires so that there is no direct contact between the wires and the cake.

• Stamens – Small bunches of stamens on fine wires form the centres of dainty flowers such as blossom. These are inserted into the centres of each sugar flower and then the flowers can be wired and wrapped in floristry tape.

Sugarcraft Equipment

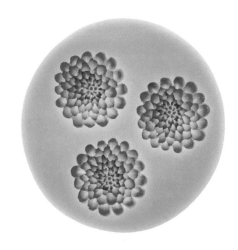

❧ Silicone Moulds – These are small moulds made in the shape of flowers, leaves, lace, etc. that can be filled with flower paste, which is then is pushed out to give an instant shaped decoration.

❧ Stamps and Cutters – Cutters for cutting out intricate icing shapes can be bought from specialist cake and baking stores. Like normal cookie cutters, they come in classic metal styles, in plastic, or as plunger-style. If you do not have appropriate cutters, there are some templates at the back of this book that can be used instead.

You will need a selection of flower cutters made from plastic or metal to cut out petals, blossom and leaves from flower paste. A good basic selection will include small, medium and large blossom cutters, a selection of daisy, star flowers and Tudor rose cutters and some basic petal and leaf cutters.

❧ Small Plastic Bottles – Small, reusable plastic storage bottles with pointed tips are handy for keeping different colours of royal icing for piping onto cookies.

❧ Ribbons – Satin or floristry paper ribbons give each cake a flourish and can cover over any mistakes or defects.

❧ Print Wrap – Patterns can be printed on edible paper or rice paper. Edible printed ribbons can be bought from cake decorating specialists.

❧ Edible-Ink Pens – Small, felt-tipped pens with edible food colouring are useful for marking faces or tiny details onto sugarpaste models.

Sugarpaste Tools

∼ Balling Tool – A balling tool (directly right) is invaluable for making rounded shapes and impressions.

∼ Boning Tool – A boning tool (directly right) has a large and a smaller rounded and curved end. These will help you to model hollow shapes in balls of sugarpaste, or curved cup shapes in petals and flowers.

∼ Fluting Tool – A fluting tool (directly right) creates open centres in cut-out shapes.

∼ Scriber Needle – A scriber needle or pin tool (directly right) is used for marking out lettering or patterns on your cake.

∼ Quilting Tool – A quilting tool is needed for straight lines and stitching effects.

∼ Cutting Wheel – This is used for cutting sugarpaste and flower paste in a wide variety of patterns. You can use a crimped edge pasta cutting wheel for a crimped effect.

∼ Crimping Tools – Operated like tweezers, crimpers with different edges give finishes such as heart shapes, curved swags and quilted-line effects, often around the edge of a cake.

∼ Flower Nail – A flower nail (bottom right in the picture on the right) is used for making piped royal iced or buttercream flowers. A square of waxed paper is attached to the 'head' of the 'nail' and the nail is turned as the petals are piped out onto the paper.

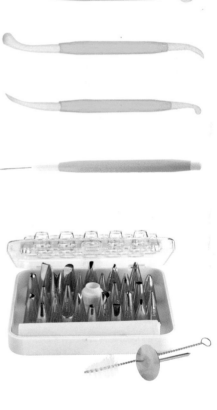

      Sugarcraft Equipment

Piping Bags and Nozzles

- **Fabric Bags** – A nylon piping bag that comes with a set of five nozzles is a very useful piece of equipment for decorating with icings. Look for a set with a plain nozzle and various star nozzles for piping swirls. The larger the star nozzle, the wider the swirls will be on the finished cake. Nylon piping bags can be washed out in warm soapy water and dried out, ready to re-use again and again.

- **Disposable Bags** – Paper or clear plastic icing bags are available and are quick and easy to use. Clear plastic piping bags are useful for piping large swirls on cup cakes.

- **Make a Paper Icing Bag** – Cut out a 38 x 25.5 cm/15 x 10 inch rectangle of greaseproof paper. Fold it diagonally in half to form 2 triangular shapes. Cut along the fold line to make 2 triangles. One of these triangles can be used another time – it is quicker and easier to make two at a time from one square than to measure and mark out a triangle on a sheet of paper.

Fold one of the points on the long side of the triangle over the top to make a sharp cone and hold in the centre. Fold the other sharp end of the triangle over the cone. Hold all the points together at the back of the cone, keeping the pointed end sharp. Turn the points inside the top edge, fold over to make a crease, then secure with a piece of sticky tape.

To use, snip away the end, place a piping nozzle in position and fill the bag with icing, or fill the bag with icing first, then snip away a tiny hole at the end for piping a plain edge, writing or piping tiny dots.

Sugarcraft Techniques

Covering a Cake with Almond Paste

Almond paste (*see* page 42) gives a base layer over which to cover a cake with icing, giving a smooth, flat surface that encloses the cake and keeps it moist. Rich fruit cakes need to be covered in almond paste to cover the dark cake and improve its keeping qualities.

First, remove all the papers in which the cake was baked, and trim the top of the cake level if it has peaked. Brush the top and sides of the cake with apricot glaze (*see* page 42).

Sprinkle a clean flat surface with icing sugar and knead one third of the almond paste. Roll out to the same shape as the top of the cake and lay the paste on top.

Measure the circumference of the cake or the length of one side with a piece of string. Knead the remaining paste and, using the string as a guide, roll the paste into a strip long enough to go round the cake and wide enough to cover the sides. Roll the paste up into a coil and press one end onto the side of the cake. Unroll the paste, pressing into the sides of the cake as you go round. Press the top and sides together to join them.

Flatten the top and sides with a small rolling pin or an icing smoother and leave to dry out for 24 hours before icing and decorating.

Using Buttercream and Cream Cheese Frostings

These soft icings can be swirled onto the tops of cakes with a small palette knife or placed in a piping bag fitted with a star nozzle to pipe impressive whirls, such as when you want to finish off your cake with a piped border or simply add those elegant flourishes.

Keep cakes with frostings in a cool place, or refrigerate, as they contain a high percentage of butter, which will melt easily in too warm a place.

~ Covering a Cake with Frosting – Do not be mean with the amount of frosting you use. If this is scraped on thinly, you will see the cake underneath, so be generous.

If your cake has a dark crumb base, such as a chocolate cake, place it in the freezer for 15 minutes before spreading over the buttercream, to give a firm base that will keep the crumbs from spreading into the buttercream.

Place a generous amount in the centre of the cake and spread this over the top with a large, flat-bladed knife or a palette knife. Spread over the sides separately and tidy up the edges with an icing scraper.

~ Piping Buttercream onto Cupcakes – Take a large piping bag and add the nozzle of your choice. A star nozzle will give a whirly effect and a plain nozzle will create a smooth coiled effect. Half fill the bag, shake down the buttercream and fill the bag again. Twist the top round to seal tightly. Squeeze the bag until the buttercream comes out. Start on the outer edge and gently squeeze the buttercream out in one continuous spiral. Lift the bag away to give a peaked finish to the top.

~ Decorating Buttercream – Cakes coated in buttercream can be decorated easily with colourful sprinkles and sugars. This is easy

Sugarcraft Techniques

with cupcakes. Place the sprinkles in a small saucer or on a piece of nonstick baking parchment and roll the outside edges of each cupcake in the decorations.

Using Sugarpaste

Sugarpaste is a versatile icing, as it can be used for covering whole cakes or modelling all sorts of fancy decorations.

- Paste food colourings are best for working with sugarpaste and a little goes a very long way. As these are very concentrated, use a cocktail stick to add dots of paste gradually, until you are sure of the colour, and knead in until even.

- Always roll out almond paste or sugarpaste on a surface lightly dusted with icing sugar. Use cornflour for rolling out flower paste as this needs to be kept dry and flexible.

- Leave sugarpaste-covered cakes to firm up for 2 hours before adding decorations, as this provides a good finished surface to work on.

- Once decorated, store sugarpaste-covered cakes and biscuits in large boxes in a cool place. Do not store in a refrigerator, as the sugarpaste will become damp and colours may run.

- Covering a Large Cake with Sugarpaste Icing – If covered in almond paste, brush the paste lightly with a little boiled water, or, if using buttercream or apricot glaze, spread these over the trimmed cake to give a surface for the sugarpaste to stick to.

Knead the sugarpaste until softened, then roll into a ball. Roll out to about 1 cm/$\frac{1}{2}$ inch thickness on a flat surface lightly dusted with icing sugar, moving the sugarpaste occasionally to prevent it from sticking to the surface.

Take a piece of string and measure the distance across the top and down either side of the cake and cut the sugarpaste 2.5 cm/1 inch larger in order to cover the whole cake. Lift the sugarpaste carefully onto the cake, holding it flat with your palms until it is central.

Dust your hands with icing sugar and smooth the icing down over the top and sides of the cake, fluting out the bottom edges. Do not pleat the icing, as this will leave lines. Smooth down to remove any air bubbles under the surface of the icing, then trim the edges with a sharp knife.

Using the flat of your hand or an icing smoother, flatten out the top and sides using a circular movement. Do not wear any rings, as these will leave ridges in the soft icing. Gather up the trimmings into a ball and keep these tightly wrapped in a plastic bag.

☙ To Cover Cupcakes – Cut out circles the size of the cupcake tops. Coat each cake with a little apricot glaze or buttercream and press on the circles to form a flat surface.

☙ Decorating Biscuits with Sugarpaste – This is one of the easiest ways to decorate cookies and it will give a great finish in less time than piping on icing. Simply roll out the sugarpaste thinly and cut out the design using the same cutter used to cut out the dough. Spread the cookie

with a little royal icing and use this to stick the sugarpaste shape on. Press down and neaten the sides with a sharp knife. Pipe on patterns with a little royal icing, or stick on sprinkles and sugarpaste shapes to decorate.

❧ To Copy Patterns from the Templates onto Sugarpaste – At the back of this book, you will find templates for some of the shapes used in the recipes. Trace the pattern you want onto a sheet of clear greaseproof paper or nonstick baking parchment. Roll out the sugarpaste thinly, then position the traced pattern on top. Mark over the pattern with the tip of a small sharp knife or a pin. Remove the paper and cut out the marked-on pattern with a small sharp knife.

❧ Making Flat Decorations – To make letters, numbers or flat decorations, roll out the sugarpaste thinly and cut out the shapes. Leave to dry on nonstick baking parchment on a flat surface or a tray for 2–3 hours to make them firm and easy to handle.

❧ Making Bows – Roll out the sugarpaste thinly on a surface lightly dusted with icing sugar and, with a knife, cut out long, thin narrow strips.

Roll small squares of baking parchment into narrow tubes, or line the handle of a wooden spoon with clingfilm. Fold the icing over the paper or handle to form loops and leave to dry and harden for 2 hours, then carefully remove the paper or spoon handle.

To make bows that are placed directly onto the cake, fill the centre of each loop with cotton wool balls, then remove these when the icing is firm.

Sugarcraft Basics

Making Roses – Colour the sugarpaste icing with pink paste food colouring. Take a small piece of sugarpaste and make a small cone shape, then roll a small pea-size piece of sugarpaste into a ball. Flatten out the ball into a petal shape and wrap this round the cone shape.

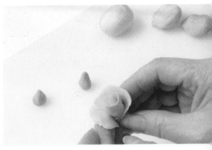

Continue adding more petals, then trim the thick base. Leave to dry for 2 hours in a clean egg box lined with foil or clingfilm.

Making Lilies – Lilies of all sizes and colours can make elegant decorations for cakes (*see* Cala Lilies Wedding Cake, page 198 for example).

Colour a little sugarpaste a deep yellow and mould this into thin sausage shapes. Leave these to firm on nonstick baking parchment or clingfilm for 2 hours.

Thinly roll out white sugarpaste and mark out small squares of 4 x 4 cm/1 ^{1}/$_2$ x 1 ^{1}/$_2$ inches. Wrap each square round a yellow centre to form a lily and press the end together. Place the lilies on nonstick baking parchment to dry out for 2 hours.

Making Daisies – Daisies of all sizes are a popular flower to be found on decorated cakes.

To model from sugarpaste, roll out a little sugarpaste thinly and, using a daisy stamp cutter, press out small flower shapes and mould these into a curve.

Leave the daisies to dry out on nonstick baking parchment, then pipe dots into the centre of each one with yellow royal icing or a small gel tube of writing icing.

Sugarcraft Techniques

Making Butterfly Wings – Colour the sugarpaste and roll out thinly. Trace round the butterfly patterns and cut out the wing shapes. Leave these to dry flat on nonstick baking parchment for 4 hours to make them firm and easy to lift.

Making Ruffles – To make frills and ruffles, roll out the sugarpaste on a surface lightly dusted with icing sugar and stamp out a fluted circle 6 cm/2¹/₂ inches wide with a pastry cutter. Cut away a small plain disc 2.5 cm/1 inch wide from the centre, and discard. Take a cocktail stick and roll this back and forth until the sugarpaste begins to frill up.

Using Silicone Moulds – Push-up silicone moulds have made cake decorating so easy as all you have to do is press a little sugarpaste into the mould and then press this out and you will have a beautiful ready-made decoration. You can buy these moulds online from sugarcraft specialists or from hobby and craft shops. You will find a huge selection in all sorts of shapes and sizes – flowers, borders, buttons, toys and novelties of all types.

To make a moulded shape, roll out a pea-size ball of sugarpaste on a surface dusted with icing sugar until pliable. Make sure the mould is clean and dry and dust it with a little icing sugar. Gently push the paste into the mould. Don't force it too hard or it will clog the mould. Turn the mould over and flex it until the sugarpaste shape drops out. Repeat until you have the number of shapes needed, then leave these to dry out overnight on a sheet of nonstick baking parchment.

Using Embossing Tools and Mats to Decorate – Embossing tools make lacy impressions and designs on sugarpaste. These come as stamps or plastic strips with a raised impression and are pushed into the soft paste to make the pattern. They can be used in conjunction with lustre powders to make a two-tone effect.

Using Royal Icing

- **Covering a Cake with Royal Icing** – Make sure the almond paste has dried out for 24 hours, or oil from the paste may seep into the icing. Place a large spoonful of icing in the centre of the cake and smooth out using a palette knife in a paddling movement to get rid of any air bubbles.

Draw an icing rule across the top of the cake towards you at an angle. Repeat, pulling back and forth, until the icing is flat. Remove any surplus icing round the top edges and leave to dry out for 24 hours. Keep the remaining icing covered in an airtight plastic box. To cover the sides, for best results, place the cake on an icing turntable. Spread a layer of icing round the sides, using the same paddling motion as for the top. Smooth the surface roughly, then, holding an icing scraper at a 45-degree angle, rotate the cake, keeping the scraper still. Rotate the cake until the sides are flat, then carefully lift away any excess icing with a palette knife to give a clean top edge. Leave to dry out for 24 hours. Repeat, adding another layer of icing to give a smooth surface for decorating.

- **Piping Royal Icing Borders** – Fit a small paper icing bag with a star or a straight nozzle and fill the bag three-quarters full with royal icing. Fold over the top and push out a little of the icing at right angles to the base of the cake. As the icing is pushed out, reduce the pressure and lift the bag away. Continue piping another shape next to the first one, until you have completed the border round the base of the cake. You can use the same technique for piping buttercream onto cakes, but this will be a little softer to pipe out and requires less pressure.

- **Piping Flowers on a Flower Nail** – Cut small squares of waxed paper and attach each to a flower nail with a dot of royal icing.

To pipe a rose, half fill a small piping bag fitted with a flower nozzle and, holding the nozzle with the thinnest part uppermost, pipe a small cone onto the paper to form the rosebud. Pipe petals round the rosebud onto the paper, overlapping each one and curling the edge

Sugarcraft Techniques

away. Leave the roses to dry out for 12 hours, then peel away from the paper to use, or store in an airtight container between layers of baking parchment until needed.

To pipe a daisy, work with the thick edge of the nozzle towards the centre and pipe five even-sized petals so that they meet in a star shape. Pipe a round dot in the centre in a contrasting colour and leave to dry out as above.

Decorating Biscuits with Royal Icing – Using glossy royal icing on cookies really gives them a professional finish. The best finish will be achieved by using packet royal icing mix, as this can easily be made into a flooding consistency.

You will first need to outline the edge of the cookie or pipe on a design with a firm-consistency royal icing. Place the icing in a piping bag fitted with a no 2 plain nozzle and pipe round the outline, making a firm join to finish. Make the flooding icing to the consistency of runny honey by adding a few drops of water. Make up all the colours you need and place these in different piping bags or small plastic bottles with snip tops. Wait for the outline to dry, then flood with icing. If you are using more than two colours, you will need to let each colour dry or they will blend into each other. You can, however, drag a cocktail stick through two colours to give a marbled or feathered effect.

Using Glacé Icing

A quick and easy way to cover cakes and cookies is by using glacé icing. This is just a paste made from icing sugar and water until a coating consistency is formed. Liquid or paste food colourings can be added to glacé and it needs to be used immediately, as it will start to set once spread. Add any sprinkles or decorations to the wet glacé icing immediately, or sprinkle over chopped nuts or cherries.

To make a feathered effect in glacé icing, colour one batch of icing, then colour a little icing in a contrasting colour and place this in a small paper icing bag. Spread the main colour over the cake or cookie and then pipe a pattern onto the wet icing and pull a wooden toothpick through this immediately to give a feathered effect. Work quickly while the icing is wet and then leave to dry and set for 1 hour.

Using Chocolate

∾ Melting Chocolate – Care and attention is needed to melt chocolate for baking and cake decorating needs. If the chocolate gets too hot or comes into contact with water or steam, it will 'seize' or stiffen and form into a hard ball instead of a smooth melted mixture. You can add a little vegetable oil or margarine, a teaspoon at a time, to the mixture to make it liquid again.

To melt chocolate, break the bar into small pieces, or grate or chop it, and place in a heatproof bowl standing over a bowl of warm, not hot, water. Make sure the bowl containing the chocolate is completely dry and that steam or water cannot enter 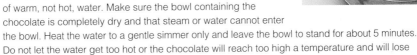 the bowl. Heat the water to a gentle simmer only and leave the bowl to stand for about 5 minutes. Do not let the water get too hot or the chocolate will reach too high a temperature and will lose its sheen.

The microwave oven is ideal for melting chocolate. Place the chocolate pieces in a small microwave-proof bowl and melt gently on low or defrost settings in small bursts of 30 seconds, checking and stirring in between, until the chocolate has melted.

Sugarcraft Techniques

Covering Cupcakes with Melted Chocolate – If the cakes have domes, trim them neatly. While the chocolate is still warm, pour a little over each cupcake. Take each cake and gently tap on a surface to spread the icing to the edges of the cases. Add sprinkles or decorations and leave to set for 1 hour.

Covering a Cake with Chocolate – Trim the cake level if necessary then place on a wire rack over a tray. Pour the warm melted chocolate over and, working quickly, spread the chocolate over the top and sides with a palette knife. Patch up any bare areas and leave to set for 1 hour. Add any decorations while the icing is still wet and leave to dry.

Curls – To make curls, melt the chocolate following your preferred method and then spread it in a thin layer over a cool surface, such as a marble slab, ceramic tile or piece of granite. Leave until just set but not hard. Take a clean paint scraper and set it at an angle to the surface of the chocolate, then push, taking a layer off the surface. This will curl until you release the pressure.

Caraque – Caraque are long thin curls. To make caraque, prepare the chocolate in the same way as for the curls. Use a large, sharp knife and hold it at about a 45-degree angle to the chocolate. Hold the handle and the tip and scrape the knife towards you, pulling the handle but keeping the tip more or less in the same place. This method makes thinner, tighter, longer curls.

Shaved Chocolate – Using a vegetable peeler, shave a thick block of chocolate to make mini curls. These are best achieved if the chocolate is a little soft, otherwise it has a tendency to break into little flakes.

- Chocolate Shapes – Spread a thin layer of chocolate, as described in the instructions for chocolate curls, and allow to set as before. Use shaped cutters or a sharp knife to cut out shapes. Use to decorate your cakes.

Finishing Touches

You will find a huge selection of cake accessories in craft and hobby shops or online. These include edible jewels made from sugar, which add sparkle to large and small cakes. Edible pearls and diamonds can set off a wedding cake or more fun edible jewels can be a favourite for children's party cakes.

- Glitter comes in bright colours in pots and is sold as dust or granules with a shine. Dusting powders give a more subtle natural sheen to flowers and ribbons.

- Printed papers and ribbons made from edible rice paper can create a pretty effect and can be cut through when serving the cake.

- Cupcake paper liners made from cut-out paper lace can be wrapped around deep cupcakes for a special occasion.

- Ribbons and paper lace trims can be found in abundance in craft and hobby shops or online cake decorating suppliers. A colourful contrasting or toning ribbon will set off a cake beautifully. Tie ribbons round the finished cake and secure them with a dab of royal icing. Never use pins on a cake.

- Crystallising Petals, Leaves and Berries – Wash and dry herbs and leaves such as rosemary sprigs and small bay

Sugarcraft Techniques

leaves or berries such as cranberries. Separate edible petals from small flowers such as rosebuds and clean small flowers such as violets with a clean brush, but do not wash them. Beat 1 medium egg white with 2 tsp cold water until frothy. Paint a thin layer of egg white carefully over the items, then sprinkle lightly with caster sugar (*see* picture page 77), shaking to remove any excess. Leave to dry on a wire rack lined with nonstick baking parchment.

Stacking Tiered Cakes

For large tiered cakes, you will need to insert small sticks of wooden or plastic dowelling into the lower tiers to take the weight of the next layer and stop it sinking.

First decide where you need to position the dowels: cover the cake with almond paste and sugarpaste and place centrally on a board. Place a sheet of baking parchment over the cake, cut to the size of the top of the cake. Based on the size of the cake that is to stand on top, decide where you want the dowels to go and mark four equal dots in a square, centrally on the paper.

Replace the paper and mark through each dot with a skewer. Remove the paper and push a dowel down into the cake at each mark. Make a mark with a pencil on the dowel at the point where the dowel comes out of the cake. Pull the dowels out of the cake and, using a serrated knife, trim them to 1 mm/^{1}/$_{32}$ inch above the pencil mark. Replace the dowels in the cake and ensure these are all 1 mm above the surface of the cake. If not, trim them again, then place the next tier of the cake on top (this should be sitting on a thin cake board that fits its size). Repeat if using three tiers.

If you are going to transport a tiered cake, remember to take each tier in a separate cardboard cake box and assemble it at the venue. Do not ever think of trying to transport a tiered cake once it is stacked up – it will be too heavy and you may damage all your hard work.

Seasonal

Sugarcraft

Once you understand the techniques, sugarcraft can be used to make your cakes, cookies, cupcakes and cake pops suit any seasonal occasion. From spring and Easter through to Halloween and Christmas, this section offers a wealth of seasonal sugarcraft projects. Try your hand at the adorable Spring Daffodil Cupcakes or the delicious Easter Egg Cake Pops and, for a festive activity to enjoy with children, the Gingerbread House will not disappoint!

Spring Daffodil Cupcakes

Makes 12

For the cakes:

1 batch lemon cupcakes
(*see* page 34)

To decorate:

1 batch lemon buttercream
225 g/8 oz ready-to-roll
sugarpaste
yellow, green and orange paste
food colourings
icing sugar, for dusting

Trim the tops of the cakes flat if they have peaked slightly. Place the buttercream in a large piping bag fitted with a star nozzle.

Colour half the sugarpaste pale yellow, a quarter green and a quarter pale orange. Roll out the yellow paste on a small board or surface lightly dusted with icing sugar. Using a small petal cutter, stamp out 24 sets of petals. Using a bone tool, make an indentation in each petal and leave to dry on a sheet of nonstick baking parchment.

Mould the orange icing into 24 pea-size balls, then press this into a cone shape round the bone tool. Flatten out slightly, then dampen the underside of the cone lightly with a little cold boiled water and stick into the centre of a set of petals. Continue to make 24 sets of petals.

Roll the green sugarpaste into long thin strips on a surface dusted with icing sugar, then cut into 24 short lengths for the stems.

Pipe the buttercream onto the cakes in large swirls, then place the petals in the icing in six sets of three flowers and six sets of a single flower. Position the green stems as shown in the picture.

Spring Cupcakes

Serves 12

For the cakes:

1 batch chocolate cupcakes
(*see* page 34)

To decorate:

75 g/3 oz ready-to-roll sugarpaste
yellow and green paste
food colourings
icing sugar, for dusting
1 batch vanilla buttercream
18 bought sugar violet flowers
6 bought large pink piped
sugar flowers
6 bought rice paper flowers
18 tiny bought sugar Easter eggs

Colour the sugarpaste pale yellow and roll out on a surface lightly dusted with icing sugar. Using a Tudor rose cutter, stamp out six yellow daisy shapes and leave to dry out on a sheet of nonstick baking parchment.

Colour the buttercream pale green with a little paste food colouring, then place in a piping bag fitted with a small star nozzle. Pipe the buttercream onto each cake in a swirl.

Place the yellow daisies onto six cakes and decorate these with the sugar violets and the pink sugar flowers.

Place the rice paper daisies on the six remaining cakes and decorate these with the sugar Easter eggs.

Easter Egg Cake Pops

Makes 12

12 unbaked vanilla cake pops
(*see* page 37)

To decorate:

1/2 batch vanilla buttercream
700 g/11/2 lb ready-to-roll
sugarpaste
pink, yellow, blue, orange and
green paste food colourings
12 thin lollipop sticks
block floristry foam
1/2 batch royal icing
(*see* page 52)

Take each cake pop and roll it lightly between your palms to make an oval shape. Coat each cake pop thickly in buttercream, then place on a baking tray.

Divide the sugarpaste into 12 pieces and colour three pink, three yellow and three blue. Take a pink piece of sugarpaste and roll this into a ball. Using a small plastic rolling pin, roll the ball out to a circle large enough to cover the oval shape. Drape the sugarpaste over the oval shape, trim and press the joins together until smooth. Roll the oval between your palms to make a smooth finish.

Repeat the covering and rolling process until all the ovals are covered, then place them on the lollipop sticks and place them in the floristry foam to keep them secure and upright.

Divide the royal icing into four batches and colour orange, light blue, yellow and leave one batch white. Place each batch in a small paper icing bag fitted with a no 1 plain nozzle and pipe on wiggly lines, hearts, daisies and small blossom flowers as shown in the picture.

Easter Bunny Cupcakes

Makes 12

For the cakes:

1 batch chocolate cupcakes
(*see* page 34)

To decorate:

green, brown, pink, blue,
yellow, orange and
black paste food colourings
¹/₂ batch vanilla buttercream
900 g/2 lb ready-to-roll sugarpaste

Colour the buttercream bright green with a little paste food colouring. Trim the tops of the cakes if they have peaked, then spread the buttercream over them. Colour 125 g/4 oz sugarpaste bright green and divide into small balls. Place a ball in an icing press or garlic press and push the sugarpaste through until it comes out in strands. Place the strands in the green buttercream to represent grass, repeat and cover all the cakes.

Leave 175 g/6 oz sugarpaste white, colour 350 g/12 oz brown, 75 g/3 oz pink, 75 g/3 oz light blue, 75 g/3 oz mid-blue and 75 g/3 oz deep pink. To make the rabbit, roll a small ball of brown sugarpaste for the body and a smaller round for the head. Model two brown ears and stick to the back of the head with a little cold boiled water. Roll two small sausages for the arms and flatten out for the paws. Roll two more sausage shapes for the feet and press the ends flat. Decorate the face and front by modelling rounds of white sugarpaste as shown, a small pink button nose and, from leftover scraps of sugarpaste, two black eyes with dots of white sugarpaste, then stick to the face and front with a little cold boiled water.

Position the body, arms and feet on the cake and stick in place with a little cold boiled water. Decorate the feet with tiny pink patches. Roll the light blue, mid-blue and pink sugarpaste into 36 tiny oval egg shapes. Colour scraps yellow and orange and roll into tiny balls with any other scraps. Decorate the eggs with dots and position three on each cake.

Easter Egg Cookies

Makes 20–24

For the cakes:

1 batch butter-rich cookie dough
(*see* page 35)

To decorate:

1 batch royal icing (*see* page 52)
pink, blue and yellow paste
food colourings

Roll out the dough and cut into ovals with a cutter, or follow the template on page 253. Bake as instructed on page 35 and leave to cool.

Place a plain no 2 nozzle in a small paper icing bag and fill the bag with plain white icing. Pipe an outline right round the edge of each cookie, making a neat join, and leave the cookies to dry for 5 minutes.

Divide the icing into two bowls and keep one bowl covered with clingfilm. Add a few drops water at a time to the other bowl to make a thinner, pourable consistency. Place the white icing in a paper icing bag and snip away the end. Gently pipe the white icing into the outline on each cookie to flood it. Leave to dry, perfectly flat, for 2–3 hours.

Divide the reserved icing into three batches and colour them pink, blue and yellow. Place each batch in a small paper icing bag fitted with a no 1 plain nozzle.

When the white-coated cookies are perfectly dry, pipe on flowers and dots with the blue icing, lines and dots with the yellow icing and squiggles and dots with the pink icing as shown in the picture. Leave to dry, perfectly flat, for 1 hour.

Halloween Ghost Cake Pops

Makes 12

12 baked and cooled vanilla
cake pops (*see* page 37)

To decorate:

1/2 batch vanilla buttercream
12 thin lollipop sticks
block floral foam
350 g/12 oz ready-to-roll
sugarpaste
icing sugar, for dusting
black paste food colouring

Spread the cake pops all over with a layer of buttercream. Place a lollipop stick firmly in the base of each cake, then arrange the sticks in a block of floral foam to keep them upright.

Make the ghosts. Divide the sugarpaste into twelve 25 g/1 oz balls, then roll each one out to an 11 cm/4 1/4 inch circle on a surface lightly dusted with icing sugar. Lift each circle over a cake pop and smooth over the top, leaving the edges loosely draped.

Re-roll the trimmings and colour black with paste food colouring. Roll two tiny black circles for each cake for the eyes and a larger one for the mouth.

Dampen the discs underneath lightly with cold boiled, water then stick them in place on the white icing to form faces. Leave the cake pops standing upright in the floral block, as this is a good way of keeping them secure.

Witch's Hat Halloween Cupcakes

Makes 12

For the cakes:

1 batch chocolate cupcakes
(see page 34)

To decorate:

1 batch cream cheese frosting
(see page 46)
orange, yellow and black paste
food colourings
450 g/1 lb ready-to-roll sugarpaste
black sugar sprinkles

Colour the cream cheese frosting bright orange with a little paste food colouring and place in a piping bag fitted with a star nozzle. Pipe a large swirl on top of each cake.

Colour 40 g/1¹/₂ oz sugarpaste orange and 15 g/¹/₂ oz yellow. Colour the remaining sugarpaste black. To model the witch's hats, divide the black sugarpaste into 12 equal pieces. Roll each piece into a pointed cone, curve the top over, then pinch out the base between your fingers to form a flat edge.

Place the hats on a sheet of nonstick baking parchment. Roll the orange sugarpaste into a thin sausage, then roll with a small rolling pin to flatten this out. Cut into 12 lengths, each long enough to fit round the base of a hat.

Dampen the underside of each strip lightly with cold boiled water and stick around the hats. Roll out the yellow sugarpaste thinly and cut into 12 small squares. Cut out the centre of each square and very carefully stick the yellow buckle onto the hat trim. Place the hats on the orange frosting just before serving and scatter over the black sugar sprinkles.

Halloween Cookies

Makes 24

For the cookies:

1 batch butter-rich cookie dough
(*see* page 35)

To decorate:

1¹/₂ batches royal icing
(*see* page 52)
green, orange and black paste
food colourings

Roll out the dough and stamp out using cutters, or cut round the templates on page 253, six ghosts, six pumpkins and six cats. Carefully place on baking sheets and bake as instructed on page 35. Cool on a wire rack.

Colour 2 tbsp of the icing green, then leave one third white, colour one third orange and one third black with paste food colouring.

Place the white icing in a small paper bag fitted with a no 2 plain nozzle. Pipe a thin line all round the outside of the ghost biscuits, making a neat join, then leave to dry for 5 minutes. Thin down the remaining white icing with a few drops water to make a pouring consistency then flood inside the outline so that the icing covers the cookies. Repeat the outlining and flooding with the orange icing to decorate the pumpkins and the black icing to decorate the cats. Leave all the cookies to dry for 2 hours.

Finish the decorations. Place the remaining black icing in a piping bag fitted with a no 1 plain nozzle and pipe faces on the ghosts, then pipe outlines for eyes, noses and mouths onto the orange icing and fill in the shapes. Place a little white icing in a bag fitted with a no 0 nozzle and pipe eyes, nose and whiskers on the cats' faces. Finish the pumpkins by placing the green icing in a piping bag fitted with a no 2 plain nozzle and pipe on the green stalks. Leave to dry for 1 hour.

Snowman Cupcakes

Makes 8

For the cakes:
8 bought chocolate cupcake cases

For the snowmen:
100 g/3¹/2 oz dark chocolate, melted
125 g/4 oz fruit cake, crumbled
125 g/4 oz vanilla sponge cake,
crumbled
2 tbsp desiccated coconut
25 g/1 oz glacé cherries,
finely chopped
1 tbsp sweet sherry or orange juice

To decorate:
700 g/1¹/2 lb ready-to-roll sugarpaste
icing sugar, for dusting
3 tbsp apricot glaze (see page 42)
red, blue and black paste
food colourings
granulated sugar, for rolling
small striped mint sweets

Place the melted chocolate and all the remaining snowman truffle cake ingredients in a bowl and stir together until well combined. Roll into golf ball-size pieces and chill for 1 hour until firm.

Roll half the sugarpaste out thinly on a surface lightly dusted with icing sugar, then cut out circles large enough to cover the balls. Brush the cake balls with a little apricot glaze, then gather the icing up round each to cover it. Press the joins neatly, place underneath and roll the ball in your palms to smooth. Roll eight small balls for the heads, then colour the scraps red and model some of the scraps into hats.

Colour a little sugarpaste blue and roll into a thin sausage. Roll a white strand similarly and then roll the two together to make a stripy rope. Repeat with the remaining red scraps and white sugarpaste. Roll each body part in granulated sugar, then place in a chocolate cupcake case. Position the blue stripy ropes, then stick on the heads with a little cold boiled water. Wrap the red stripy scarves around the necks and attach 2 stripy sweets on the front as buttons. Mark two black dots as eyes on the head, attach a scrap of red icing for a nose and mark on a happy mouth with a skewer.

Festive Cake Pops

Makes 12

For the cakes:

12 baked vanilla cake pops
(*see* page 37)

To decorate:

$^1/_2$ batch vanilla buttercream
700 g/1$^1/_2$ lb ready-to-roll
sugarpaste
red paste food colouring
12 thin lollipop sticks
thin satin red ribbon
block floristry foam in a red paper
gift container
$^1/_2$ batch royal icing
(*see* page 52)
shredded clear wrapping

Coat each cake pop thickly in buttercream, then place on a baking tray.

Colour the sugarpaste bright red and divide the sugarpaste into 12 pieces. Take a piece of sugarpaste and roll this into a ball. Using a small plastic rolling pin, roll the ball out to a circle large enough to cover the round shape.

Drape the sugarpaste over the round, trim and press the joins together until smooth. Roll between your palms to make a smooth finish.

Repeat the covering and rolling process until all the rounds are covered, then place them on the lollipop sticks, Tie a red ribbon around the sticks and place them in the floristry foam to keep them secure and upright.

Make the royal icing into a smooth piping consistency by adding a few drops water if necessary. Place the royal icing in a paper icing bag fitted with a no 1 plain nozzle. Holding a cake pop by the stick, decorate the ball with piped lines, then add small dots to make them into sprig decorations. Pipe on all 12 cake pops, then leave them to dry in the floristry foam in the red box. Decorate the top of the box with shredded clear wrapping for a festive touch.

Christmas Cookies

Makes 12

For the cookies:

1 batch butter-rich cookie dough
(*see* page 35)

To decorate:

500 g/1 lb 1 oz ready-to-roll
sugarpaste
red and green paste
food colourings
¹/₂ batch royal icing
(*see* page 52)
small silver and gold sprinkles
edible liquid gold colouring
red and gold dragees

Roll out the dough and cut out, using the templates on page 252 if liked, four each of the fir trees, cupcakes and mittens. With any spare dough, cut out snowflakes freehand. Carefully place on baking sheets and bake as instructed on page 35. Cool on a wire rack. Colour one third of the sugarpaste red, one third green and leave the rest white. Spread the cookies with a little royal icing.

Make the fir trees: roll out the green sugarpaste and cut out to fit over the cookies, reserving the scraps. Press down and mark a border round the outer edge. Make a 'pot' for the tree with white icing and press in place. Colour a little royal icing green, place in a paper bag fitted with a no 2 plain nozzle and pipe a swirl as shown. Scatter gold and silver sprinkles onto the wet icing. Paint the 'pot' with liquid gold, then paint a star on top of the tree.

Make the cupcakes: roll out the red and white sugarpaste and cut out the top and base shapes. Stick in position as shown. Colour one third of the remaining royal icing red. Place the remaining white icing in a paper piping bag fitted with a no 1 plain nozzle. Pipe small white swirls on top of the cupcake and place a red dragee in each one. Place a little red icing in a paper icing bag and pipe lines on the base. Decorate with a gold dragee and holly leaves made from green sugarpaste scraps.

Make the mittens: pipe a red outline round the outer edges of the cookie. Make the remaining red icing into a flooding consistency with a few drops water. Pipe the icing into the mitten shape, then pipe white stripes across. Draw a toothpick through the white icing to make a feathered effect. Leave to dry for 1 hour. Finish the base with a scrap of red sugarpaste marked with a skewer to make a ribbed effect. Model a bow from white sugarpaste scraps and finish with a little gold paint.

For snowflakes, roll out the remaining white sugarpaste, cut out the shapes and press onto the cookies. Pipe on white sprigs of royal icing.

Chocolate Christmas Cupcakes

Makes 8

For the cakes:
8 bought chocolate cupcake cases

For the filling:
100 g/3^1/$_2$ oz dark chocolate, melted
125 g/4 oz fruit cake, crumbled
125 g/4 oz vanilla sponge
cake, crumbled
2 tbsp desiccated coconut
25 g/1 oz glacé cherries,
finely chopped
1 tbsp dark rum or orange juice

To decorate:
450 g/1 lb chocolate covering icing
(see page 56)
icing sugar, for dusting
3 tbsp apricot glaze
125 g/4 oz ready-to-roll sugarpaste
red and green paste food colourings
small bought chocolate decorations

Place the melted chocolate and all the remaining truffle cake ingredients in a bowl and stir together until well combined. Roll into golf ball-size pieces and chill for 1 hour until firm.

Roll the chocolate covering out thinly on a surface lightly dusted with icing sugar and cut out circles large enough to cover the balls. Brush the cake balls with a little apricot glaze, then gather the icing up round each to cover it. Press the joins neatly together, place underneath and roll the ball in your palms to smooth. Place the balls in the chocolate cupcake cases.

Colour 50 g/2 oz of the sugarpaste red, 25 g/1 oz green and leave 25 g/1 oz white. Roll half the red sugarpaste into a thin sausage and repeat with the white sugarpaste. Roll the two strands together to make a stripy rope. Cut into eight lengths and bend the end of each piece round to make a candy cane shape. Leave to firm on nonstick baking parchment for 1 hour. Roll the remaining red sugarpaste into 24 small berries and leave to dry on the baking parchment.

Roll out the green icing thinly, then, using leaf cutters and veiners, make 16 small leaves. When firm, stick the berries, leaves and canes in place with a little cold boiled water and decorate the chocolate cases with chocolate shapes.

Gingerbread House

For the house:

1 batch gingerbread dough
(*see* page 36)

To decorate:

1¹/₂ batches royal icing
125 g/4 oz white chocolate buttons
75 g/3 oz ready-to-roll sugarpaste
red and green paste
food colourings
icing sugar, for dusting
silver and coloured metallic
dragees, and red sprinkles
granulated sugar, for sprinkling

Roll out the dough and, using the templates on page 244, cut out roof pieces, sides, gables and chimney pieces. Bake and cool as instructed on page 36. When cool and stiff, assemble the house on a cake board. Fill a large piping bag fitted with a no 3 plain nozzle with royal icing and pipe along the wall edges. Join the walls together on a cake board and leave to set. Pipe along the top gable and wall edges and position the roof. Pipe around the chimney pieces, place these at the back of the roof and leave to set.

Pipe dots of royal icing onto the roof and fix on the chocolate buttons in an overlapping pattern. Colour the sugarpaste red and roll out thinly on a surface lightly dusted with icing sugar. Cut out a small door and four shutters, then mark lines on with a knife. Stick the door and shutters in place with royal icing. Pipe hearts on the shutters and door and decorate the door with a silver dragee. Pipe lines and dots around the door and shutters, across the rooftop and chimney to decorate as shown in the picture. Pipe thick lines on the corner joins of the gables, then pipe onto the roof edges, letting the icing flick down to represent icicles. Spread white royal icing onto the cake board around the base of the house, flicking up to represent snow. Scatter over sparkly granulated sugar.

Place a little white icing in a paper icing bag fitted with a leaf nozzle. Starting at the base, pipe leaf shapes in a circle, pipe on another layer of smaller leaves, then continue building up the layers to make a fir tree. Colour the remaining icing green and pipe two green trees. Decorate the trees with silver dragees while still wet. Pipe leaf shapes either side of the door and scatter with red sprinkles while still wet.

Tea Party

Pretty

If there's one occasion where sugarcraft comes into its own like no other, it would have to be a tea party! If you want to offer a tempting array of beautiful and colourful treats which seem almost too good to eat, then look no further than this section. The Chocolate Bonbons Cake makes a superb tea party centrepiece, whilst Teatime Cake Pops and Colourful Flower Cookies will delight both adults and children alike.

Delicate Daisy Pearl Cake

Serves 10

For the cake base:

1 Madeira sponge cake baked in a
2 litre/4 pint bowl (*see* page 32)
and covered in almond paste
(*see* page 42)

To decorate:

125 g/4 oz flower paste
pink, yellow and turquoise paste
food colourings
cornflour, for dusting
granulated sugar, for sprinkling
875 g/1³/₄ lb ready-to-roll
sugarpaste
icing sugar, for dusting
edible pearl decorations
pink ribbon trim

Colour three quarters of the flower paste pale pink and the rest pale yellow. Roll out the pink flower paste thinly on a small board or surface lightly dusted with cornflour and, using a large daisy cutter, stamp out a daisy. Roll along each of the petals with a bone tool to make them separate and to curl up the edges. Leave the daisy to dry on crumpled foil for 3–4 hours until firm. Model a small, round centre with the yellow paste, dampen the underside with a little boiled water and place in the centre of the daisy, then sprinkle with a little granulated sugar.

Colour the sugarpaste pale turquoise with a little paste food colouring and roll out on a surface lightly dusted with icing sugar to a circle large enough to cover the domed cake. Brush the almond paste lightly with cold boiled water and drape the sugarpaste over. Smooth down over the top and sides, then trim round the base.

Lightly dampen the top of the cake with a little cold boiled water, then place the daisy on top. Press the edible pearls into the sides of the cake, pushing into the sugarpaste while it is still flexible. Trim the base with a thin pink ribbon to finish.

Birds & Scrolls Cupcakes

Makes 12

For the cakes:

1 batch vanilla cupcakes
(*see* page 34)
2 tbsp apricot glaze

To decorate:

700 g/1¹/₂ lb ready-to-roll sugarpaste
pink and blue paste food colourings
icing sugar, for dusting
edible gold lustre powder

Colour 225 g/8 oz of the sugarpaste pink and the remainder deep blue. Make 12 small pink roses, following the instructions on page 71 and leave them to dry out in empty egg boxes lined with crumpled foil.

Trim the cupcakes to give them a rounded shape and brush the glaze over. Roll out the blue sugarpaste thinly on a surface lightly dusted with icing sugar. Using a round cutter, stamp out 12 circles, 6 cm/ 2¹/₂ inches wide.

Dust the inside of an embossing pattern mould lightly with gold powder and flick away the excess with a soft paintbrush. Press the circle of sugarpaste into the mould, pressing around the pattern, then lift it out carefully and drape the blue icing over the cupcake. Press the icing in position, being careful not to touch the gold design. Repeat with the remaining cakes, leaving three plain for contrast.

To finish the cakes, trim the base of each rose flat and dampen with a little cold boiled water. Stick the roses in position just before serving.

Lemon Roses Cake

Serves 12-14

For the cake base:

1 x 20 cm/8 in round Madeira cake
(see page 32)
3 tbsp apricot glaze

To decorate:

550 g/1¼ lb ready-to-roll sugarpaste
icing sugar, for dusting
350 g/12 oz flower paste
yellow and green paste
food colourings
cornflour, for dusting
gold lustre powder
1 tbsp royal icing
yellow satin ribbon trim

Trim the top of the cake if it has peaked and brush the apricot glaze over the top and sides of the cake.

Knead the white sugarpaste into a round ball and flatten out. Roll out on a surface lightly dusted with icing sugar to a circle large enough to cover the top and sides of the cake. Using both hands, carefully lift over the cake and smooth down over the top and sides. Trim away the edges, then place the cake on a 25 cm/10 inch cake board or flat serving plate.

Colour three quarters of the flower paste yellow and one quarter green. Model the yellow paste into three large open roses and four small buds (see page 71) and leave these to firm for 3 hours in egg boxes lined with crumpled foil. Roll the green flower paste out on a surface lightly dusted with cornflour and cut out three large leaves with a leaf cutter. Press on veins with a veining mould and use a sharp knife to mark them on. Leave to dry and firm for 3 hours.

Dust the ends of the leaves with a little gold powder, then arrange the flowers, buds and leaves on the cake, attaching them with a dab of royal icing. Arrange a lemon satin ribbon around the base of the cake.

Simple Lilac Cupcakes

Makes 12

For the cakes:

1 batch chocolate cupcakes
(*see* page 34)

To decorate:

blue and pink paste food
colourings (optional)
700 g/1¹/₂ lb royal icing (optional)
12 lilac blue piped sugar flowers
6 large pink piped sugar flowers
6 large white piped sugar flowers
6 bought blue rice paper flowers
¹/₂ batch cream cheese frosting
(*see* page 46)

Colour the royal icing, then place in piping bags fitted with a small petal nozzle and pipe sugar flowers onto squares of waxed paper. Leave to dry according to the instructions on page 73, or you will find a wide selection of colourful ready-made flowers on sale in the supermarket.

Place the cream cheese frosting in a large piping bag fitted with a star nozzle and pipe swirls on the chocolate cakes.

Place a lilac blue flower in the frosting on each cake, then attach a large pink daisy on top of six cakes.

Place a white sugar flower and a blue rice paper flower in the frosting on the remaining six cakes. Serve within 2 hours, or the colours from the sugar flowers may start to spread into the frosting.

Strawberries Roses Cupcakes

Makes 12

For the cakes:

1 batch vanilla cupcakes
(*see* page 34)

To decorate:

900 g/2 lb ready-to-roll sugarpaste
green, pink, red and blue paste
food colourings
$^1/_2$ batch vanilla buttercream
icing sugar, for dusting

Colour 50 g/2 oz sugarpaste green, then divide the rest into four pieces and colour one half dark and half light pink, one red, one blue and keep one white. Trim the cakes if necessary, then spread with a thin buttercream layer.

Make four large and 12 small strawberries: roll a piece of red sugarpaste into an oval shape, pinch the end, flatten out slightly, then mark with a skewer. Take a little of the pink sugarpaste and roll into a 9 x 2.5 cm/3$^1/_3$ x 1 inch strip. Wind the strip around one end to make a simple coiled rose. Make 12 small pale pink roses and 24 darker pink roses. Trim the bases so they will sit flat. Model the green sugarpaste into four large and 12 small green leafy tops for the strawberries and press them on. Make 12 green leaves, pinch the centres. Leave all to dry for 1 hour.

Roll 50 g/2 oz white sugarpaste thinly on a surface dusted with icing sugar and cut out four white Tudor rose petal shapes. Roll out the remaining white sugarpaste thinly and cut into strips 5 mm/$^1/_4$ inch wide. Repeat making strips with the remaining pale pink sugarpaste and half the blue sugarpaste. Place alternate strips of pink and white on four cakes, and blue and white on four cakes. Trim the edges neatly and smooth together. Roll out the blue sugarpaste thinly and cut into discs, 6 cm/2$^1/_2$ inches wide. Place on four cupcakes, smooth on, then mark on a square pattern with a knife. Top with the white Tudor rose petal shapes. Arrange the strawberries and roses on the cakes as shown, fixing with a little cold boiled water.

Pink Sugar Rolled Daisy Cupcakes

Makes 12

For the cakes:

1 batch vanilla cupcakes
(*see* page 34)

To decorate:

125 g/4 oz ready-to-roll sugarpaste
pink paste food colouring
icing sugar, for dusting
1 batch vanilla buttercream
25 g/1 oz granulated sugar

Colour 25 g/1 oz sugarpaste pink, then roll out the remainder on a small board or surface lightly dusted with icing sugar and cut out 12 daisies using a medium daisy cutter. Mould the pink sugarpaste into 12 small balls and mark the centre of each with the tip of a small knife to represent the centre of a flower. Press the petals upwards to curl them, then lightly dampen the underside of each pink centre and press into the daisies. Leave to dry for 1 hour on nonstick baking parchment.

Colour the buttercream pale pink and colour the granulated sugar a deeper shade of pink with a little pink paste food colouring. Place the pink buttercream in a large piping bag fitted with a plain nozzle. Pipe a plain swirl around the outside of each cupcake, then fill in the centre by piping a large round swirl.

Just before serving, spread the pink sugar out onto a saucer and dip the outside of each cake in the sugar, lightly coating round all the sides. Place a daisy in the centre of each cake to finish.

Tea Party Cupcakes

Makes 12

For the cakes:

1 batch vanilla cupcakes
(*see* page 34)

To decorate:

700 g/1 1/2 lb ready-to-roll sugarpaste
blue, pink and green paste
food colourings
1/2 batch vanilla buttercream
icing sugar, for dusting
tiny pink edible metallic balls
edible liquid gold colouring

Colour 50 g/2 oz of the sugarpaste light blue, 25 g/1 oz pink, 25 g/1 oz dark pink and 25 g/1 oz green. Trim the tops of the cakes completely flat, then lightly coat with the buttercream.

Roll out half the white sugarpaste thinly and cut into circles 10 cm/4 inches wide. Roll the edges of each circle with a toothpick to flute them up. Press an embossing tool onto each circle to make the impression of a pattern. Lift each circle carefully and lay onto each cake to make the tablecloth. Roll out the blue sugarpaste on a surface lightly dusted with icing sugar and cut into small squares to fit the top of each cake. Mark again with the embossing tool, then score the outer edges with a sharp knife to make a border. Dampen the underside of each square with a little cold boiled water and place on the tablecloths.

Mould 12 small plates, 12 saucers, 12 cups, 12 teapots and 12 spoons from the white sugarpaste. Shape the pink sugarpaste into 36 tiny cakes and make a white top for each one, then press in a pink metallic ball to finish. Model pink scraps into three coiled roses and green scraps into three tiny leaves, dampen and press onto the teapot. Leave for 1 hour to firm on nonstick baking parchment.

Decorate the spoon, edges of the plates, cup, saucer and teapot with gold paint on the tip of a fine paintbrush. Arrange everything as shown.

Dainty Daisy Cookies

Makes 24

For the cookies:

1 batch basic cookie dough
(*see* page 35)

To decorate:

900 g/2 lb ready-to-roll sugarpaste
lilac, pink, mint green and yellow
paste food colourings
icing sugar, for dusting
1/2 batch royal icing
(*see* page 52)
edible metallic coloured balls
caster sugar, for sprinkling

Roll out the dough and cut into petal shapes with a cutter, or follow the template on page 248. Bake as instructed on page 35 and leave to cool.

Divide the sugarpaste into four portions. Colour one quarter lilac, one pale pink and one rose pink. Divide the remaining sugarpaste into three portions and colour one third mint green, one third yellow and leave one third white.

Roll out the lilac sugarpaste on a surface lightly dusted with icing sugar and cut out eight daisy shapes following the template, to fit over the cookies. Spread a cookie with a little royal icing, then position and press the sugarpaste onto the cookie to stick to the edges. Continue until you have covered the remaining cookies with all the lilac and pink sugarpastes.

Roll out the yellow, green and white sugarpastes thinly on a surface dusted with icing sugar. Use a blossom cutter to cut out small blossom flowers to decorate the centres of the cookies.

Place the remaining royal icing in a paper icing bag fitted with a no 1 straight nozzle. Position the coloured blossom flowers in the centres of the cookies and secure with a small blob of royal icing. Pipe on lines and dots to decorate as shown. Position the metallic balls in the centres of the flowers and push into the icing. Sprinkle the centres with a little caster sugar to serve.

Blue Daisy Cupcakes

Makes 12

For the cakes:

1 batch vanilla cupcakes
(*see* page 34)
3 tbsp apricot glaze

To decorate:

700 g/1¹/₂ lb ready-to-roll
sugarpaste
blue and yellow paste food
colourings
icing sugar, for dusting
¹/₄ batch royal icing
tiny gold and silver seed sprinkles

Colour 125 g/4 oz of the sugarpaste blue, cover in clingfilm and reserve. Trim the cupcakes to give them a flat top and brush the apricot glaze over.

Roll out the white sugarpaste thinly on a surface lightly dusted with icing sugar. Using a round cutter, stamp out 12 circles 6 cm/2¹/₂ inches wide, then press down with an embossing tool to make a raised pattern in the icing. Stick the discs onto the tops of the cakes.

Gather up the white scraps and roll out thinly. Stamp out 12 large star flowers, 12 medium star flowers, 24 small star flowers and 24 small blossom flowers with cutters. Place the medium star flowers in the large star flower shapes. Shape the flowers to curve the petals with a small bone tool.

Roll out the blue sugarpaste on a small board or surface lightly dusted with icing sugar. Stamp put 80 large blossom flowers, 80 medium and 80 small blossom flowers with blossom cutters. Colour the royal icing a pale yellow and place in a paper icing bag fitted with a no 0 plain nozzle. Pipe small dots into the centres of the blue flowers.

Attach the flowers around the outer edge of each cake with a dot of royal icing. Arrange the gold and silver seeds in the centres of the white flowers, then arrange on top of the cake as shown.

Romantic Rose Cupcakes

Makes 12

For the cakes:

1 batch vanilla cupcakes
(*see* page 34)

To decorate:

225 g/8 oz ready-to-roll
sugarpaste
pink paste food colouring
granulated sugar
1 batch vanilla buttercream

Colour the sugarpaste pale pink. Colour the granulated sugar pink, then spread out onto a saucer and reserve.

Roll the pink sugarpaste until flexible, then take a pea-size ball and roll into a cone shape. Take another ball and flatten out into a petal shape. Wrap the petal around the cone and continue to add petals to make an open rose (*see* page 71). Trim the base and leave to dry in an egg box lined with crumpled foil for 2 hours to firm. Make 12 roses.

Place the buttercream in a large piping bag fitted with a star nozzle. Pipe the buttercream onto the cakes in large swirls, then place a rose in the centre of each swirl. Scatter over the pink sugar just before serving.

Marzipan Fruits

Makes 16

450 g/1 lb bought yellow almond
paste or home-made almond
paste (*see* page 42)
whole cloves
red, yellow, green, orange and
purple paste food colourings

To make the apples: take one quarter of the almond paste, then roll a small piece into a ball. Make an indentation in the top, take a clove and press this in to represent the stalk. Take a medium-size paintbrush and lightly stipple red colouring over to represent the skin of the apple. Leave on a sheet of nonstick baking parchment to dry for 1 hour.

To make the pears: take one quarter of the almond paste and colour yellow. Take a small piece and make a ball, then mould it into a tapered pear shape between your fingertips. Make an indentation in the top and press in a clove for the stalk. Lightly stipple it with green colouring. Leave on paper to dry for 1 hour.

To make the peaches: take one quarter of the almond paste and colour light orange. Roll into small balls and lightly stipple with red and orange food colouring. Indent with a skewer and leave on paper to dry for 1 hour.

To make the plums: take one quarter of the almond paste and colour mid-purple. Roll into small ovals and lightly stipple with purple food colouring. Leave on a sheet of nonstick baking parchment to dry for 1 hour.

Note: If you have an airbrushing machine, this can be used with liquid food colourings to create the stippled skin effects on the fruits more easily.

Teatime Cake Pops

Makes 12

For the cakes:

12 baked vanilla cake pops
(see page 37)

To decorate:

700 g/1¹/₂ lb ready-to-roll
sugarpaste
blue and yellow paste food
colourings
¹/₂ batch vanilla buttercream
12 thin lollipop sticks
block floristry foam
small seed pearl decorations
¹/₄ batch royal icing

Colour 125 g/4 oz of the sugarpaste yellow. Colour the remainder blue and divide into 12 pieces. Make four teapots: take a piece of blue sugarpaste and roll this into a ball. Using a small plastic rolling pin, roll the ball out to a circle large enough to cover the round shapes. Coat 4 cake pops thickly in buttercream, drape the sugarpaste over, trim and press the joins together until smooth. Press a short, thick sausage of blue sugarpaste onto one side and shape into the spout, smoothing to join. Make a ball, flatten out and stick in place on top with a little cold boiled water for the lid. Add a tiny ball for the handle. Model a small, thin sausage to make the handle, curve round and stick in place. Make a small round for the lid and stick in place. Place the teapots on the lollipop sticks and place them in the floristry foam to keep them upright.

Make eight teacups: trim across the tops of 8 cake pops to make a flat surface. Trim round the sides to make cup shapes, then trim the bases flat. Coat the 8 cake pops thickly in buttercream, cover with strips and circles of rolled blue sugarpaste, trim and press the joins together until smooth and flatten out the top and base. Model a small sausage of blue icing to make the handle, curve round and stick in place. Make a small round for the saucer and stick in place. Place the teacups on the lollipop sticks and place them in the floristry foam.

Roll out the yellow icing thinly, stamp out small and medium blossom shapes and stick onto the teapots and cups. Decorate the flowers, sides and lids with seed pearls as shown, sticking with small dabs of royal icing.

Magenta Rose Cupcakes

Makes 12

For the cakes:

1 batch lemon cupcakes (*see* page 34)

To decorate:

1 batch lemon buttercream
225 g/8 oz ready-to-roll sugarpaste
magenta pink and green paste food colourings
icing sugar, for dusting
narrow magenta pink satin ribbon

Trim the tops of the cakes flat if they have peaked slightly. Place the buttercream in a large piping bag fitted with a star nozzle.

Colour three quarters of the sugarpaste magenta pink and the remainder leaf green. Roll out the green paste on a small board or surface lightly dusted with icing sugar. Using a small-size leaf cutter, stamp out 12 leaf shapes. Mark on veins with a sharp knife and leave to dry on a sheet of nonstick baking parchment for 1 hour.

Knead the magenta sugarpaste until flexible, then take a pea-size ball and roll into a cone shape. Take another ball and flatten out into a petal shape. Wrap the petal around the cone and continue to add petals to make a small rose (*see* page 71). Trim the base and leave to dry in an egg box lined with crumpled foil for 2 hours to firm. Make 12 roses.

Pipe the buttercream onto the cakes in large swirls, then place a rose and leaf on each, in the icing as shown. Tie a length of narrow satin ribbon around each cake and finish with a bow.

Colourful Flower Cookies

Makes 24

For the cookies:

1 batch butter-rich cookie dough
(*see* page 35)

To decorate:

900 g/2 lb ready-to-roll sugarpaste
green, pink, blue and yellow paste
food colourings
icing sugar, for dusting
$1/2$ batch royal icing
coloured sprinkles in blue
and yellow
caster sugar, for sprinkling

Roll out the dough and cut into flower shapes with a cutter, or follow the templates on page 248. Bake as instructed on page 35 and leave to cool.

Divide the sugarpaste into three portions. Colour one third lime green, one pink and one blue.

Roll out the green sugarpaste on a surface lightly dusted with icing sugar and cut out eight flower shapes, following the templates, to fit over the cookies. Spread a cookie with a little royal icing and position, then press the sugarpaste onto the cookie to stick to the edges. Continue until you have covered the remaining cookies with the pink and blue sugarpastes.

Colour the remaining royal icing in four batches: pink, blue and green to match the sugarpaste covering, and yellow. Place a batch of icing in a paper icing bag fitted with a no 1 straight nozzle and pipe lines round each petal, then decorate with dots and lines as shown in the picture. Pipe a round into the centre of each cookie and fill with dots of royal icing. Scatter the coloured sprinkles onto the icing in the centre in a contrasting colour, then sprinkle lightly with caster sugar. Repeat with the remaining icing and colours.

Yellow Daisy Swag Cake

Serves 12–14

For the cake base:

1 x 20 cm/8 in round lemon
Madeira cake (*see* page 32)

To decorate:

¼ batch lemon buttercream
900 g/2 lb ready-to-roll sugarpaste
yellow paste food colouring
icing sugar, for dusting

Trim the top of the cake flat if it has peaked and spread the buttercream over the top and sides of the cake. Colour 700 g/1½ lb sugarpaste yellow. Cut away 50 g/2 oz and roll the rest into a ball and flatten out. Roll out on a surface lightly dusted with icing sugar to a circle large enough to cover the top and sides of the cake. Using both hands, carefully lift over the cake and smooth down over the top and sides. Trim away the excess edges then place the cake on a 25 cm/10 inch cake board or flat serving plate.

Roll out the remaining white sugarpaste on a surface lightly dusted with icing sugar. Cut out a large daisy shape and mark between the petals with a skewer. Roll a long, thin strip, measuring 2 x 127 cm/¾ x 50 inches. Brush round the base of the cake lightly with a little boiled water then stick the strip to the sides in loose pleats.

Roll out a yellow strip, 14 x 23 cm/5½ x 9 inches, thinly on a surface lightly dusted with icing sugar and press on a pattern with an embossing tool. Take one end of the strip and gather together. Dampen the cake lightly and stick in place, draping over the cake as shown. Place the white daisy shape on top of the pleated end. Roll a yellow disc for the daisy centre and stick in place.

Roll out the white sugarpaste scraps and, using a small flower cutter, cut out about 30 small shapes. Dampen each lightly with cold boiled water, then stick onto the yellow icing to finish.

Butterfly Cupcakes

Makes 12

For the cakes:

1 batch chocolate cupcakes
(*see* page 34)

To decorate:

1 batch vanilla buttercream
green, black and blue paste
food colourings
175 g/6 oz ready-to-roll
sugarpaste
icing sugar, for dusting
coloured sprinkles

Trim the top of each cake flat if they have peaked slightly. Colour the buttercream lime green, then place in a large piping bag fitted with a star nozzle.

Colour one quarter of the sugarpaste black and colour the remainder blue. Roll the black icing into 12 small sausage shapes. Pinch each end to make an oval, then mark with a knife to make the head and body of the butterfly. Roll out the blue sugarpaste thinly on a surface lightly dusted with icing sugar and cut out 12 pairs of wings with a cutter or follow the template on page 251. Press a pattern onto the wings with an embossing tool, or mark with a skewer.

Place 1 teaspoon water in a cup and add a dot of blue paste colouring. Stir to blend, then lightly paint onto the outside of each wing to decorate.

Pipe the buttercream onto the cakes in stars, then place a coloured sprinkle on each star point. Arrange two butterfly wings in the icing and then position the body part in the centre.

Dots Daisies Mini Cakes

Makes 8 mini cakes

For the cakes:

1 batch vanilla cupcake mix
baked in individual 5 cm/2 inch
round mini cake moulds
(see page 34)

To decorate:

1/2 batch vanilla buttercream
875 g/1³/4 lb ready-to-roll
sugarpaste
yellow paste food colouring
icing sugar, for dusting
1/4 batch royal icing
narrow white ribbon trim

Trim the top of each cake flat if they have peaked, then stand flat so the domed part is upright. Spread the buttercream over the tops and sides of the cakes.

Reserve 125 g/4 oz of the white sugarpaste, then colour the remainder a pale yellow. Divide the yellow paste into eight pieces and roll out on a surface lightly dusted with icing sugar. Drape over each cake and smooth down over the top and sides to remove any pleats. Trim the bases neatly, then smooth with your hands to make a neat finish.

Roll out the white sugarpaste on a surface lightly dusted with icing sugar, then cut out 40 small flower shapes using a four-petal flower cutter. Curve and shape the petals outwards and leave to dry on nonstick baking parchment for 1 hour to firm.

Place the royal icing in a small paper icing bag fitted with a no 1 plain nozzle. Pipe dots as centres in the flowers, then pipe dots around the base of each cake as shown. Attach five flowers to each cake as shown with a blob of royal icing, then attach a ribbon around the base of each cake to serve.

Chocolate Bonbons Cake

Serves 24

For the cake base:

1 x 25 cm/10 inch round chocolate
cake (*see* page 31)

To decorate:

2 tbsp orange liqueur or
orange juice
1 batch vanilla buttercream
900 g/2 lb ready-to-roll sugarpaste
cream and brown paste
food colourings
icing sugar, for dusting
125 g/4 oz white chocolate, melted
30 dark chocolate truffles
125 g/4 oz toasted chopped
hazlenuts

Trim the top of the cake flat if it has peaked. Beat the orange liqueur or juice into the buttercream. Cut the cake in half horizontally and spread with a little buttercream, then replace the top and spread buttercream over the top and sides of the cake.

Colour three quarters of the sugarpaste pale cream with a little paste food colouring, then roll out the sugarpaste on a surface lightly dusted with icing sugar to a circle large enough to cover the cake. Carefully lift this over the cake, then smooth down and trim away the edges.

Colour the scraps and remaining sugarpaste light brown. Roll out thinly on a surface lightly dusted with icing sugar and, using a pasta wheel, cut out thin strips 1 cm/$^1/_2$ inch wide. Brush the underside of the fluted strips with a little cold boiled water and stick around the sides of the cake at regular intervals. Trim the tops of the strips level with a sharp knife.

Place the melted white chocolate in a small paper icing bag. Snip a small hole at the top and pipe whirls round 10 of the truffles. Spread a little of the remaining melted chocolate over 10 more truffles and roll them in chopped hazelnuts. Place the chocolates alternately in plain, chopped nuts and whirl patterns around the base of the cake. Arrange 9 truffles on top of the cake as shown.

Garden of Flowers Cupcakes

Makes 12

For the cakes:

1 batch chocolate cupcakes
(*see* page 34)

To decorate:

$^1/_2$ batch vanilla buttercream
green paste food colouring
225 g/8 oz ready-to-roll
sugarpaste
$^1/_4$ batch royal icing
36 piped royal iced flowers
(*see* page 73),OR
12 bought red sugar flowers
12 bought cream sugar flowers
12 bought pink sugar flowers
yellow sugar seed sprinkles

Colour the buttercream bright green with a little paste food colouring. Trim the tops of the cakes if they have peaked, then spread the buttercream over them.

Colour the sugarpaste bright green and divide into small balls. Place a ball in an icing press or garlic press and push the sugarpaste until it comes out in strands. Place the strands in the green buttercream to represent grass, repeat and cover all the cakes.

Place a small dab of royal icing in the centre of each sugar flower and sprinkle over the yellow sugar seeds to make stamen centres. Dab each sugar flower underneath with a little royal icing and arrange a pink, red and cream flower on top of each cake.

Butterfly Trio Cupcakes

Makes 12

For the cakes:

1 batch vanilla cupcakes
(*see* page 34)

To decorate:

1 batch vanilla buttercream
350 g/12 oz ready-to-roll sugarpaste
cream and pink paste
food colourings
icing sugar, for dusting
gold lustre powder
edible gold star sprinkles

Trim the top of each cake flat if they have peaked slightly. Place the buttercream in a large piping bag fitted with a star nozzle. Colour half the sugarpaste pale cream, one quarter dark pink and one quarter pale pink.

Roll the cream sugarpaste out thinly on a surface lightly dusted with icing sugar and cut out 12 large butterflies with a cutter, or follow the template on page 251. Press a pattern onto the wings with an embossing tool, or mark on with a skewer. Repeat using the deep pink sugarpaste to make 12 medium-size butterflies and the pale pink sugarpaste to make 12 smaller ones. Tilt the wings upwards and leave to dry between two open folded sheets of nonstick baking parchment for 2 hours to firm.

Dust the cream butterflies with a little gold powder, applied with a dry paintbrush.

Pipe the buttercream onto the cakes in large swirls, then scatter with the gold star sprinkles. Arrange a large, medium and small butterfly on each cake to serve.

Pink Blue Flower Cupcakes

Makes 12

For the cakes:

1 batch vanilla cupcakes
(*see* page 34)
2 tbsp apricot glaze

To decorate:

450 g/1 lb ready-to-roll sugarpaste
pink and pale turquoise paste
food colourings
icing sugar, for dusting
125 g/4 oz flower paste
cornflour, for dusting
edible seed pearl decorations
light pink and magenta dusting
powders

Trim the cupcakes to give them a flat surface and brush the apricot glaze over.

Colour the sugarpaste pale turquoise, then roll out thinly on a surface lightly dusted with icing sugar. Using a fluted cutter, stamp out 12 circles, 6 cm/2^1/$_2$ inches wide. Stick the discs onto the cakes and smooth out lightly with your fingertips. Take a quilting tool and mark lines across in two directions to make diamond shapes. Decorate six cakes with a quilted pattern and leave six plain.

Colour the flower paste pink and roll out very thinly on a small board dusted with cornflour. Using a daisy cutter, cut out four daisies, curl up the edges with a balling tool and press a seed pearl in the centre of each flower. Repeat making four flowers with an open flower cutter and 4 with a four-petal flower cutter. Dust the edges of the petals of the open flower with magenta dusting powder and lightly brush the others with light pink dusting powder. Leave to dry out on a sheet of nonstick baking parchment for 1 hour.

To finish, place the open flowers on the quilted patterned cakes and the other eight on the plain cakes. Dampen the centre of each cake lightly with a cold little boiled water, then press the flower in place.

Celebrations ✺ Special Occasions

A homemade and personally decorated cake is a lovely and heartfelt gesture for a special occasion. Whether it be a wedding, christening or someone's birthday, this section offers projects for all of these occasions and more. For an impressive cake which will cater for a large party, try the Tiered Rose Petal Cake, whilst the Sea Shells Wedding Cake is stunning for any wedding. If you are looking for an original gift idea, a batch of New Baby Cookies are a perfect pick-me-up for new parents.

Tiered Rose Petal Cake

Serves 80–100

For the cake base:

1 each 15 cm/6 inch, 20 cm/8 inch
and 25 cm/10 inch round rich fruit
cakes, covered in almond paste
(*see* pages 28 and 42)

To decorate:

2.25 kg/5 lb ready-to-roll sugarpaste
450 g/1 lb flower paste
light and deeper pink paste food
colourings
cornflour, for dusting
1/2 batch royal icing

Divide the sugarpaste into 1 kg/2¹/₄ lb, 700 g/1¹/₂ lb and 450 g/1 lb batches. Knead each batch until soft, then roll out to circles large enough to cover the top and sides of each cake. Place the large cake on a 35 cm/ 14 inch round cake drum. Place the medium cake on a thin, 20 cm/8 inch round board and the small cake on a thin, 15 cm/6 inch cake board. Brush the almond paste with a little cold boiled water, then cover each cake with the appropriate sugarpaste circles as per the instructions on page 68.

Push four sticks of wooden or plastic dowelling, cut to the depth of the cake, evenly into the large cake base. Repeat with the medium cake. These will take the weight of the cake layers. Stack the cakes on top of each other.

Colour three quarters of the flower paste pale pink and one quarter deeper pink. Roll out the pink paste thinly on a surface lightly dusted with cornflour. Cut out 50 large, 50 medium and 50 small petals using petal cutters. Curl the petals and leave to dry in egg boxes lined with crumpled foil until firm. Use the deeper pink paste to make 10 rose centres (*see* page 71) and leave to dry in crumpled foil in egg boxes for 24 hours.

Place a dab of royal icing on each rose petal and arrange around the sides of the cake as shown. Position the deeper pink rose centres as shown, then attach paler pink petals around the centres to build up open roses. Scatter a few petals loosely around the base to finish.

Delicate Lace Wedding Cupcakes

Makes 12

For the cakes:

1 batch almond flavoured
cupcakes (*see* page 34)
3 tbsp apricot glaze
(*see* page 42)

To decorate:

450 g/1 lb ready-to-roll sugarpaste
pale blue paste food colouring
icing sugar, for dusting
white dusting powder
$^{1}/_{4}$ batch royal icing
large and small seed pearl edible
decorations

Trim the cupcakes to give them a slightly domed surface and brush the glaze over.

Colour half the sugarpaste pale blue. Roll out the sugarpaste thinly on a surface lightly dusted with icing sugar. Using a 6 cm/2$^{1}/_{2}$ inch fluted cutter, stamp out six white and six blue circles. Leave three plain white. Dust a lacy embossing tool lightly with white dusting powder and press onto three blue discs to cover the whole disc. Repeat with three white discs. Add more dusting powder and press the pattern into half of the disc; repeat with three white discs. Stick the discs onto the cakes with your fingertips.

Roll out the remaining blue and white sugarpastes thinly. Cut out six large blue star flowers and six white. Curl up the petals with a bone tool and mark the centre with a veiner or a knife. Make 16 medium white and 16 blue star flowers in the same way. Stamp out 28 small white star flowers in each colour. Stamp out 28 small white and 28 blue blossom flowers. Leave to dry on a sheet of nonstick baking parchment for 1 hour.

To finish, place the large open flowers on the plain cakes and arrange the smaller flowers in lines and bunches on the patterned cakes. Attach the flowers with small dabs of royal icing. Place tiny dabs of royal icing in the centres of the larger flowers and decorate with the seed pearls.

Classic Couple Wedding Cake

Serves 80–100

For the cake base:

1 each 15 cm/6 inch, 20 cm/8 inch
and 25 cm/10 inch round rich fruit
cakes, covered in almond paste
(*see* pages 28 and 42)

To decorate:

3 kg/6 lb 10 oz ready-to-roll
sugarpaste
icing sugar, for dusting
$^1/_2$ batch royal icing
ivory shimmer lustre powder
seed pearl trim
450 g/1 lb flower paste
cornflour, for dusting
black, pink and light brown paste
food colourings
net fabric

Divide the sugarpaste into 1 kg/2$^1/_4$ lb, 700 g/1$^1/_2$ lb and 450 g/1 lb batches, reserving the remainder. Knead each batch until soft, then on a surface dusted with icing sugar roll out to circles large enough to cover the top and sides of each cake. Place the large cake on a 35 cm/14 inch round cake drum, the medium cake on a thin, 20 cm/8 inch round board and the small cake on a thin, 15 cm/6 inch cake board. Brush the almond paste with a little cold boiled water and cover each cake with the sugarpaste circles as per instructions on page 68.

Roll out the remaining sugarpaste thinly and cut out 18 strips 4 cm/1$^1/_2$ inches wide and long enough to go from top to bottom and partway into the centre of each cake as shown. Lightly dab the underside of each strip with royal icing and position at intervals as shown. With a dry pastry brush, lightly flick the ivory dusting powder evenly over the cake. Push four sticks of wooden or plastic dowelling, cut to the depth of the cake, evenly into the large cake base. Repeat with the medium cake. These will take the weight of the cake layers. Stack the cakes on top of each other. Place the pearl trim around the base of each tier.

Roll out a 12 cm/4$^1/_2$ inch circle of flower paste on a surface dusted with cornflour. Flute the edges, then drape over the edge of the top tier for the bride's gown. Model two white bodies. Colour a little paste black, roll into sausages for the groom's legs and feet. Colour a little paste for the skin and model the heads, bride's arms and groom's hands. Colour a little paste brown and model the hair. Secure the heads with toothpicks. Stick all the pieces together with a little royal icing and position on the top tier. Pipe on details with dots of royal icing and paint on the faces. Make a veil with a scrap of net fabric.

Baby Shower Heart

Serves 8

For the cookies:

1/2 batch butter-rich cookie dough
(*see* page 35)
plain flour, for dusting

To decorate:

450 g/1 lb ready-to-roll sugarpaste
light and deep pink paste
food colourings
icing sugar, for dusting
1/2 batch royal icing

Knead the cookie dough until soft and roll out on a lightly floured surface. Cut out a heart shape measuring 16 cm/6¹/2 inches across the widest point and 13 cm/5 inches deep from the indentation in the centre of the heart. Bake and cool as instructed on page 35.

Divide the sugarpaste into three portions. Colour one third light pink and one third a deeper shade of pink. Roll out the white sugarpaste thinly on a surface lightly dusted with icing sugar and cut out an oblong 10 cm x 3.5 cm/4 inches x 1¹/2 inches. Cut the remaining white icing into 3 cm/1¹/4 inch squares and shape a small ball into a button. Roll out the light and dark pink sugarpastes and make squares as above. Spread the cookie heart lightly with a little royal icing and stick on the pink and white squares, alternating the colours and tones. Press the edges together to make neat joins and trim the edges neatly.

Decorate the squares with embossed patterns, quilted lines and lines marked on with a knife. Position the button on a pink square. Model a light pink heart shape and place on a deep pink square and model a deep pink bow and place on a light pink square. Brush the underside of the white strip lightly with a little cold boiled water and position in the centre. Mark the edges with a quilting tool. Colour the remaining royal icing deep pink and place in a small paper icing bag with a plain no 2 nozzle. Pipe on the word 'Baby' or a name. Decorate the button and pipe on pink dots to finish.

New Baby Cookies

Makes 24

For the cookies:

1 batch butter-rich cookie dough
(*see* page 35)
plain flour, for dusting

To decorate:

1½ batches royal icing, made from
royal icing sugar mix
yellow and light and deep blue
paste food colourings

Knead the cookie dough until soft and roll out on a lightly floured surface. Cut out eight prams, eight rattles and eight baby-gro shapes following the templates on page 249. Bake and cool as instructed on page 35.

Divide the royal icing between five bowls. Leave one white and colour the rest yellow, dark yellow, light and dark blue. Fill a small paper icing bag fitted with a no 1 straight nozzle with a little of the yellow icing. Pipe an outline around the body of the pram, making a neat join. Repeat with the blue icing baby-gro shape, the dark blue icing rattle head and the white icing pram hood and rattle handle. Keep all the icing bags.

Add a few drops water to each of the bowls of icing to make a runny consistency for flooding the cookies. Place a no 2 straight nozzle in a small paper icing bag and fill with yellow icing. Pipe the icing into the pram outline, flooding and spreading it to fill in the shape. Repeat with the blue baby-gro, blue rattle head and white pram hood and rattle handle.

While the icing is still wet, pipe white dots onto the blue baby-gro and dark yellow dots into the white pram hood with the bags with the no 1 nozzles. Leave to dry for 3 hours.

With the appropriate colours of reserved icing in the same bags, decorate the cookies with piped lines and dots as shown, and pipe a duckling on the baby-gro with yellow icing.

Love Cookies

Makes 24

For the cookies:

1 batch butter-rich cookie
dough (*see* page 35)
plain flour, for dusting

To decorate:

1¹/₂ batches royal icing, made
from royal icing sugar mix
light and deep pink paste
food colourings
pink coloured granulated sugar
bought pink sugar blossom
flowers

Knead the cookie dough until soft and roll out on a lightly floured surface. Cut out six small, six medium and six large heart shapes and the letters 'LOVE', following the templates on page 246. Bake and cool as instructed on page 35.

Divide the royal icing between three bowls. Leave one white and colour the rest light and dark pink. Fill a small paper icing bag fitted with a no 1 straight nozzle with a little of the pink icing. Pipe an outline around the hearts and letters, making a neat join. Keep all the icing bags for decoration. Add a few drops water to each of the bowls of icing to make a runny consistency for flooding the cookies. Place a no 2 straight nozzle in a small paper icing bag and fill with light pink icing. Pipe the icing into some of the heart outlines, flooding and spreading it to the edges to fill in the shapes. Repeat with the dark pink icing, following the photo. Sprinkle a little pink granulated sugar onto some of the smaller cookies while still wet.

While the icing is still wet, pipe white dots onto the dark pink 'L' letter and dark pink dots onto the 'E' letter, and hearts onto some of the pale pink heart cookies with the bag with the no 1 nozzle. Leave to dry for 3 hours.

Decorate the 'O' letter with the reserved white icing with dots as shown, and stick on the sugar flowers. Decorate the 'V' letter with lines and the hearts with lacy edging as shown. Leave to dry for 1 hour.

Valentine Lovebird Cookies

Makes 24

For the cookies:

1 batch butter-rich cookie
dough (*see* page 35)
plain flour, for dusting

To decorate:

1¹/₄ batches royal icing, made
from royal icing sugar mix
deep blue and deep pink paste
food colourings

Knead the cookie dough until soft and roll out on a lightly floured surface. Cut out 24 rounds using a 7 cm/2³/₄ inch cutter. Bake and cool as instructed on page 35.

Divide the royal icing between two bowls. Colour one deep blue and one deep pink. Fill a small paper icing bag fitted with a no 1 straight nozzle with a little of the pink icing. Pipe an outline around half of the rounds, making neat joins. Keep the icing bags for decoration.

Add a few drops water to each of the bowls of icing to make a runny consistency for flooding the cookies. Place a no 2 straight nozzle in a small paper icing bag and fill with pink icing. Pipe the icing into the pink outlined cookies, flooding and spreading to the edges to fill in the shapes. Repeat with the blue outlines. Leave to dry for 3 hours.

Decorate the outer edges of the cookies with pink and blue dots with the reserved icing as shown. Pipe pink lovebirds onto the blue cookies and blue lovebirds onto the pink cookies, following the design in the photo. Leave to dry for 1 hour.

Pink & Orange Floral Wedding Cake

Serves 90

For the cake base:

1 x 13 cm/5 inch Madeira cake,
covered in almond paste
(*see* pages 32 and 42)
1 x 18 cm/7 inch Madeira cake,
covered in almond paste
1 x 25 cm/10 inch Madeira cake,
covered in almond paste

To decorate:

700 g/1½ lb flower paste
yellow, dark pink, orange and
green paste food colourings
cornflour, for dusting
6 batches vanilla buttercream
pale lemon paper ribbon

Make the flowers. Colour 125 g/4 oz of the flower paste yellow, then divide the remaining paste into three equal pieces and colour one dark pink, one orange and one green. Dust chrysanthemum flower moulds lightly with a little cornflour. Take a small ball of yellow paste and press into the centre of the mould. Press a circle of dark pink over the yellow ball and push right into the flower mould with your fingertips. Push the flower out onto a sheet of nonstick baking parchment. Repeat with the orange paste. Make seven orange and seven pink flowers. Roll the green paste until soft, press into leaf moulds and press out 30 leaves with a veined pattern. Leave all the flowers and leaves to dry for 24 hours.

Place the small cake on a thin, 15 cm/6 inch square board, the medium cake on a thin 20 cm/8 in board and the large on a 30 cm/12 inch square cake board. Push four sticks of thin wooden or plastic dowelling, cut to the depth of the cake, into the base of the large and medium cakes. Spread the buttercream over the top of each cake and smooth level with an icing rule. Spread the remaining buttercream around the sides with a palette knife and smooth flat with a smoother. Trim the top and side joins, then stack the cakes on top of each other.

Place the paper ribbon around the base of each cake and secure with buttercream. Fill a paper icing bag fitted with a no 3 plain nozzle with buttercream and pipe a lacy design onto the ribbon as shown. Arrange the flowers and leaves on the cake as shown just before serving.

Pure White Wedding Cupcakes

Serves 12

For the cakes:

1 batch almond flavoured
cupcakes (*see* page 34)
3 tbsp apricot glaze
(*see* page 42)

To decorate:

450 g/1 lb ready-to-roll sugarpaste
icing sugar, for dusting
$^1/_4$ batch royal icing
pink seed pearl edible decorations

Trim the cupcakes to give them a flat surface and brush the glaze over.

Roll out the sugarpaste thinly on a surface lightly dusted with icing sugar. Using a fluted cutter, stamp out 12 circles, 6 cm/2$^1/_2$ inches wide. Stick the discs onto the cakes with your fingertips.

Roll out the remaining sugarpaste thinly and cut out 60 small petals with a petal cutter, or roll the sugarpaste into small balls and mould each ball into a petal shape by hand. Roll 12 small balls into ovals, then flatten out into a leaf shape. Mark a vein down each leaf with a sharp knife.

Pinch each petal together at the base and place five petals onto each cake, dampen the underside lightly with a little cold boiled water and press into position.

Place the royal icing in a small paper icing bag fitted with a no 1 plain nozzle. Pipe a little icing into the centre of each flower and press on 3 seed pearls. Pipe a plain stem on each cake as shown, then attach a leaf to this to finish.

Star Flower Wedding Cake

Serves 90

For the cake base:

1 x 13 cm/5 inch square Madeira
cake, covered in almond paste
(*see* pages 32 and 42)
1 x 18 cm/7 inch square chocolate
cake, covered in almond paste
(*see* pages 31 and 42)
1 x 23 cm/9 inch square rich fruit
cake, covered in almond paste
(*see* pages 28 and 42)
1 x 25 cm/10 inch square rich fruit
cake, covered in almond paste

To decorate:

3 kg/6 lb 10 oz ready-to-roll
sugarpaste
royal blue paste food colouring
icing sugar, for dusting
ivory pearl and blue dusting powders
1 batch royal icing
white and royal blue satin ribbons
thin strings pearl trim

Colour 450 g/1 lb of the sugarpaste royal blue. Roll out thinly on a surface lightly dusted with icing sugar and, using star flower cutters, cut out 1 large, 12 medium and 12 small star flowers. Repeat with the same amount of white sugarpaste. Mould each petal of the flower with a bone tool to make a curve, then pinch the ends of the petals into points. Leave to dry on nonstick baking parchment for 3 hours. When the flowers are firm enough to handle, brush the inside of each white petal with ivory dusting powder and the blue ones with blue powder. Colour a little royal icing royal blue to match the flowers and place in a paper icing bag fitted with a no 2 plain nozzle. Pipe dots for centres in the middle of each flower as shown and leave to dry for 24 hours.

Knead the remaining sugarpaste and roll out to squares large enough to cover the top and sides of each cake. Cover the cakes as per the instructions on page 68. Trim the edges, then place the three smallest cakes each on a thin, square board 2 cm/³/₄ inch larger all round. Cover a 30 cm/12 inch square cake board with white sugarpaste and place the largest cake on it. Push four sticks of thin wooden or plastic dowelling, cut to the depth of the cakes, into the base of the large and medium cakes. Stack the cakes on top of each other, with the small one on top. Trim the base of each cake with white satin ribbon, then a double string of pearl trim. Trim around the cake board with the royal blue ribbon. Dab each flower underneath with a small blob of royal icing and attach the flowers in a cascade over one side, alternating the colours.

Sea Shells Wedding Cake

Serves 40

For the cake base:

1 x 23 cm/9 inch and 1 x 15 cm/6 inch Madeira cake, covered in almond paste (*see* pages 32 and 42)

To decorate:

2.25 kg/5 lb ready-to-roll sugarpaste
icing sugar, for dusting
turquoise, ivory and yellow paste food colourings
1/4 batch royal icing
orange and yellow dusting powders
edible pearl decorations

Cut off 200 g/7 oz sugarpaste. Roll out 125 g/4 oz thinly on a surface lightly dusted with icing sugar and, using a frangipane petal cutter, cut out five petals. Curve each petal into a round with your fingertips, then overlap all five petals and pinch together. Repeat, making 12 flowers, and leave to dry in egg boxes lined with crumpled foil. Colour 75 g/3 oz of the sugarpaste bright turquoise and, using a small mould or your fingers, shape three starfish. Leave to dry on nonstick baking parchment for 24 hours.

Colour the rest of the sugarpaste pale ivory with a few spots of paste food colouring. Divide into 700 g/1 1/2 lb and 450 g/1 lb batches. Knead them until soft, then roll each out to a circle large enough to cover the top and sides of the cakes. Cover both cakes as instructed on page 68. Spread a little royal icing on a 30 cm/12 inch cake drum, then roll out 75 g/3 oz scraps of sugarpaste thinly to cover the board. Smooth and trim the edges, then place the larger cake on the covered board. Place the smaller one on a thin, 15 cm/6 inch round cake board. Push four sticks of thin wooden or plastic dowelling, cut to the depth of the cake, into the base of the large cake. Stack the smaller cake on top.

Push small balls of ivory sugarpaste into seashell moulds and press out the shapes. Leave to dry on nonstick baking parchment for 24 hours. Roll some ivory sugarpaste into thin sausages and press around the base and middle joins. Dust the seashells with orange powder and the centres of the frangipane with yellow dusting powder, then place the pearls in the open shells. Dab the underside of each with a little royal icing and arrange on the top and sides of the cake with the starfish as shown.

Dusky Rose Tiered Heart Cake

Serves 75

For the cake base:

1 batch rich fruit cake mix for an
18 cm/7 inch round cake baked
in a 16 cm/6¹/₂ inch heart-
shaped cake tin, covered in
almond paste (*see* pages 28
and 42)
1 batch rich fruit cake mix for a
23 cm/9 inch round cake baked
in a 20 cm/8 inch heart-shaped
cake tin, covered in
almond paste

To decorate:

225 g/8 oz flower paste
green and light and rose pink
paste food colourings
cornflour, for dusting
1.5 kg/3¹/₃ lb ready-to-roll
sugarpaste
¹/₂ batch royal icing

Reserve 25 g/1 oz of the flower paste, then colour 50 g/2 oz green and the remainder in dark and lighter shades of rose pink. Roll out the green paste on a surface lightly dusted with cornflour and cut out eight leaves, then mark on veins with a veining tool or a sharp knife. Shape four large roses (*see* page 71) with the various shades of rose pink paste and leave to dry in egg boxes lined with foil for 24 hours. Roll the white flower paste and shape into six rose petals.

Colour the sugarpaste pink. Cut off 225 g/8 oz and colour this a deeper rose pink. Stack two 28 cm/11 inch round cake drums on top of each other and stick together with a little royal icing. Spread the top and sides with royal icing. Roll out 75 g/3 oz of the pale pink sugarpaste to a circle large enough to cover the top of the boards, press down and trim the edges. Roll the rose pink sugarpaste into a strip long enough to go around the sides of the boards, cut one edge straight and one edge with a cutter to make a fluted edge. Stick the strip around the boards and neaten the join. Divide the remaining sugarpaste into 700 g/1¹/₂ lb and 450 g/1 lb batches. Knead until soft, then roll out to heart shapes large enough to cover the top and sides of the cakes. Cover the cakes as per the instructions on page 68. Smooth and trim the edges, then place the larger cake on the covered board. Place the smaller one on a thin, 15 cm/6 inch heart-shaped cake board. Push four sticks of thin wooden or plastic dowelling, cut to the depth of the cake, into the base of the large cake. Stack the smaller cake on top. Colour the remaining royal icing dusty pink and place in a paper icing bag fitted with a no 2 plain nozzle. Pipe a shell border around the base of each heart cake. Attach the roses and leaves on top of the cake with dabs of royal icing and scatter the white petals to finish.

Black ❧ White Rose Cake

Serves 12–14

For the cake base:

1 x 20 cm/8 in round Madeira cake
(*see* page 32)
3 tbsp apricot glaze
(*see* page 42)

To decorate:

1.25 kg/2 ¹/₂ lb ready-to-roll
sugarpaste
icing sugar, for dusting
black paste food colouring
silver spray or lustre powder
¹/₄ batch royal icing
narrow and wide black
satin ribbons

Trim the top of the cake flat if it has peaked and brush the glaze over the top and sides of the cake. Knead 575 g/1¹/₄ lb of the white sugarpaste into a round ball and flatten out. Roll out on a surface lightly dusted with icing sugar to a circle large enough to cover the top and sides of the cake. Using both hands, carefully lift over the cake and smooth down over the top and sides. Trim around the edges, then place the cake on a cake board or flat serving plate.

Cut out a stencil from the pattern on page 245 in nonstick baking parchment and pin around the sides of the cake. Paint black food colouring directly onto the sides of the cake through the stencil. Remove the stencil carefully and leave the black colouring to dry for 3 hours.

Mould the remaining white sugarpaste into eight large open roses (*see* page 71) and leave to firm for 2–3 hours in egg boxes lined with crumpled foil. Cut out 10 leaves and mark veins on them using a sharp knife. Leave to dry and harden on nonstick baking parchment for 2 hours. When dry, spray or dust the leaves with silver colouring.

Gather up the sugarpaste trimmings and make into a mound shape. Attach the flowers and leaves to the mounded shape on top of the cake with dabs of royal icing. Trim the top and base of the cake with satin ribbons as shown.

Pretty Pink Heart Cake

Serves 12–14

For the cake base:

1 batch mixture for a 23 cm/9 in
round Madeira cake
(*see* page 32),
baked in a 20 cm/8 inch
heart-shaped tin
3 tbsp apricot glaze
(*see* page 42)

To decorate:

900 g/2 lb ready-to-roll sugarpaste
pink paste food colouring
icing sugar, for dusting
1/2 batch royal icing
silver balls

Trim the cake flat if it has peaked and brush the glaze over the top and sides of the cake. Reserve 125 g/4 oz of the white sugarpaste and colour the remainder pink. Knead 575 g/1 1/4 lb of the pink sugarpaste into a round ball and flatten out. Roll out on a surface lightly dusted with icing sugar to a heart shape large enough to cover the top and sides of the cake. Using both hands, carefully lift over the cake and smooth down over the top and sides. Trim around the edges, then place the cake on a cake board or flat serving plate.

Mould the remaining pink sugarpaste into seven large open roses (*see* page 71). Cut out two small hearts and leave to firm for 2–3 hours in egg boxes lined with crumpled foil. Using the white sugarpaste, cut out four large leaves and mark veins with a sharp knife. Leave to dry and harden on nonstick baking parchment for 2 hours. Roll out scraps of white sugarpaste thinly and cut out 14 small blossom shapes with a cutter.

Place one quarter of the royal icing in a paper icing bag fitted with a no 1 straight nozzle. Attach the roses, leaves and hearts with blobs of icing, then pipe on white stems and position the white blossom flowers as shown. Press a silver ball into the centre of each flower. Colour the remaining royal icing pink and place in a paper icing bag fitted with a leaf nozzle. Pipe a thick fluted border around the base of the cake as shown.

Mini Roses Birthday Cake

Serves 40

For the cake base:

1 x 20 cm/8 inch and 1 x 15 cm/6 inch Madeira, cake covered in almond paste (*see* pages 32 and 42)

To decorate:

1.75 kg/3^1/$_2$ lb ready-to-roll sugarpaste
yellow, red and green paste food colourings
icing sugar, for dusting
cord ribbon trim
^{1}/$_4$ batch royal icing

Cut off 450 g/1 lb of the sugarpaste and reserve. Colour the remaining sugarpaste pale lemon with a few spots of paste food colouring. Divide the sugarpaste into 700 g/1^1/$_2$ lb and 450 g/1 lb batches. Knead the largest batch until soft, then roll out on a surface lightly dusted with icing sugar to a circle large enough to cover the top and sides of the larger cake. Brush the almond paste with a little cold boiled water. Lift the sugarpaste over the cake, then smooth down over the top and sides and flatten with an icing tool or your hands. Trim away the edges, then repeat to cover the smaller cake.

Place the large cake on a 23 cm/9 inch cake drum and the smaller one on a thin, 15 cm/6 inch round cake board. Push four sticks of thin wooden or plastic dowelling, cut to the depth of the cake, into the base of the large cake. Stack the smaller cake on top of the large one. Cut the cord trimming to fit and stick around the base of each cake with dabs of royal icing.

Colour two thirds of the reserved sugarpaste red and one third pale green. Shape the red icing into thin sausage shapes, then flatten out between your fingers into strips. Coil up a small flattened strip of red paste into a spiral shape and press the base together, then cut the base flat. Repeat, making 70 small roses. Cut out 60 small green leaves and pinch the base of each together. Leave the roses and leaves to harden for 4 hours, then attach to the top and sides of the cake with the leaves with tiny spots of royal icing.

Present Cake Pops

Makes 16

For the cakes:

1 batch Madeira sponge cake mixture baked in a 20 cm/8 inch square tin (*see* page 32)

To decorate:

¹/₂ batch vanilla buttercream
900 g/2 lb ready-to-roll sugarpaste
red, blue and pink paste food colourings
icing sugar, for dusting
16 thin lollipop sticks
block floristry foam

Bake and cool the Madeira cake as directed on page 32 and cut into 16 x 5 cm/2 inch squares. Spread all over with buttercream and place on a baking tray.

Colour one third of the sugarpaste red, leave one third white, and colour half of the remaining paste blue and the other half pink.

Roll out the red sugarpaste thinly on a surface lightly dusted with icing sugar and cut into squares large enough to cover the cubes of cake. Cover each cube with red sugarpaste, trim and neaten the edges. Smooth the sugarpaste flat and neaten into a cube shape. Place each cube on a lollipop stick and then push into the floristry foam to secure. Repeat, using up all the red and white sugarpastes.

Roll out the pink and blue sugarpastes thinly and cut into thin ribbons 1 cm/¹/₂ inch wide. Roll a pasta wheel or a patterning tool along the centre of each ribbon to make a design. Brush the underside of the ribbon lightly with a little cold boiled water and stick onto the cubes to form ties and looped bows as shown.

Vintage Valentine Cookies

For the cookies:

1 batch butter-rich cookie dough
(*see* page 35)

To decorate:

900 g/2 lb ready-to-roll sugarpaste
lilac, pink, red and lime green
paste food colourings
icing sugar, for dusting
$\frac{1}{2}$ batch royal icing

Roll out the dough and cut into heart shapes with a cutter, or follow the template on page 247. Bake as instructed on page 35 and leave to cool.

Divide the sugarpaste into four portions. Colour one quarter lilac, one quarter pale pink and one quarter red. Colour half the remaining icing lime green and leave the other half white. Roll out the lilac sugarpaste on a surface lightly dusted with icing sugar and cut out eight heart shapes to fit over the cookies. Spread cookies with a little royal icing, then position and press on the sugarpaste, sticking the edges. Press with an embossing tool to make a raised lacy pattern. Continue until you have covered the remaining cookies with the lilac, pink and red sugarpastes.

Model the green sugarpaste into small leaf shapes. Shape the white icing into thin sausage shapes, then flatten out between your fingers into strips. Coil up a small flattened strip of red paste into a spiral shape and press the base together, then cut the base flat. Repeat, making 24 small roses. Repeat, making eight red roses from scraps. Roll scraps of different coloured sugarpastes out thinly and cut out small blossom flowers.

Colour one quarter of the remaining royal icing red, leaving the rest white. Place coloured royal icings in two paper icing bags fitted with no 1 straight nozzles. Stick the coloured blossom flowers in the centres of the cookies and secure with a small blob of white icing. Pipe on dots as shown.

Starry Flower Mini Cakes

Makes 8

For the cakes:

1 batch vanilla cupcake mix
baked in 8 x 5 cm/2 inch round
mini cake moulds
(*see* page 34)

To decorate:

¹/₂ batch vanilla buttercream
900 g/2 lb ready-to-roll sugarpaste
pink paste food colouring
icing sugar, for dusting
¹/₂ batch royal icing

Trim the top of each cake flat if they have peaked, then spread the buttercream over the top and sides of the cakes.

Reserve 225 g/8 oz of the sugarpaste, then colour the remainder a pale pink. Divide the pink sugarpaste into eight pieces and roll out on a surface lightly dusted with icing sugar. Drape over each cake and smooth down over the top and sides to remove any pleats. Trim the bases, then smooth with your hands to make a neat finish.

Roll out the white sugarpaste, then cut out about 40 small flower shapes for each cake, using a star flower cutter.

Place the royal icing in a small paper icing bag fitted with a no 1 plain nozzle. Pipe a dot onto the underside of each star flower and stick onto the pink icing, joining the stars together in a lacy pattern as shown. Pipe royal icing onto a sheet of waxed paper into butterfly outlines and leave to dry for 2 hours until firm. Stick two butterfly shapes onto each cake with a little royal icing to finish.

Bunting Wedding Cake

Serves 80–100

For the cake base:

1 each 15 cm/6 inch, 20 cm/8 inch
and 25 cm/10 inch round rich fruit
cakes, covered in almond paste
(*see* pages 28 and 42)

To decorate:

2.25 kg/4¹/₂ lb ready-to-roll
sugarpaste
icing sugar, for dusting
narrow white satin ribbon
¹/₂ batch royal icing
A4 edible printed papers
white silk embroidery thread

Divide the sugarpaste into 1 kg/2¹/₄ lb, 700 g/1¹/₂ lb and 450 g/1 lb batches. Knead the largest batch until soft, then roll out on a surface lightly dusted with icing sugar to a circle large enough to cover the top and sides of the 25 cm/10 inch cake. Brush the top and sides of the almond paste with a little cold boiled water, then smooth down over the top and sides and flatten with an icing tool or your hands. Repeat to cover the medium and small cakes.

Place the large cake on a 35 cm/14 inch round cake drum. Place the medium cake on a thin, 20 cm/8 inch round board and the small cake on a thin, 15 cm/6 inch cake board. Push four sticks of wooden or plastic dowelling evenly into the large cake base, cut to the depth of the cake. Repeat with the medium cake. These will take the weight of the cake layers. Stack the cakes on top of each other. Trim the base of each cake with a narrow satin ribbon.

Place the royal icing in a paper icing bag fitted with a no 2 plain nozzle. Cut the sheet of A4 edible paper in half lengthways, then fold in half again lengthways. Cut the folded paper into triangles. Stick the triangles onto the embroidery thread with dabs of royal icing. Carefully position the bunting around the cakes and stick in place with royal icing. Pipe on large dots of royal icing interspersed between the bunting and leave to dry for 2 hours.

Christening Booties Cake

Serves 12–16

For the cake base:

1 x 20 cm/8 inch and 1 x 15 cm/
6 inch rich chocolate cakes
(*see* page 31)

To decorate:

1¹/₂ batches vanilla buttercream
1.5 kg/3¹/₃ lb ready-to-roll
sugarpaste
icing sugar, for dusting
brown and blue paste food
colourings

Cut the tops of both cakes level if they have peaked, then cut each cake in half and spread one half with a little buttercream. Sandwich the cakes back together, then spread the remaining buttercream thinly over the top and sides of the cakes. Place the smaller cake on a thin, 15 cm/6 inch round cake board. Roll out 700 g/1¹/₂ lb of the sugarpaste on a surface dusted with icing sugar to a circle large enough to cover the top and sides of the large cake. Use to cover the cake as per the instructions on page 68. Trim the edges and place on a cake board or flat plate. Colour 450 g/ 1 lb of the sugarpaste brown and use to cover the small cake; place on a thin, 15 cm/6 inch cake board.

Reserve 25 g/1 oz of the white sugarpaste and colour the scraps and 225 g/8 oz of the sugarpaste blue. Roll out thinly and cut into strips 2.5 cm/ 1 inch wide. Brush the strips with a little cold boiled water and stick to the sides of the cake. Roll brown scraps into thin sausages and stick a thin strip down the side of each blue strip. Mould brown fan shapes and stick around the base as shown. Stack the small cake on top of the larger one. Place a blue strip around the base of the brown cake and shape into a bow.

Roll out the white sugarpaste and cut out a leaf shape; write on the baby's name if required. Mould the remaining blue scraps into two blue booties, mark on stitching with a skewer and trim the tops with white sugarpaste. Roll white scraps of sugarpaste into thin sausages and make shoelaces. Loop the laces into bows and place on the booties as shown.

Wedding Cake Cookies

Makes 24

For the cookies:

1 batch butter-rich cookie dough
(*see* page 35)

To decorate:

900 g/2 lb ready-to-roll sugarpaste
pink, red and rose pink paste
food colourings
icing sugar, for dusting
¹/₂ batch royal icing
edible metallic coloured balls

Roll out the dough and cut into tiered cake shapes, following the template on page 252. Bake and cool as instructed on page 35.

Divide the sugarpaste into four portions. Colour one quarter pale pink, one deep pink and one rose pink, leaving one quarter white.

Roll out the pale pink sugarpaste on a surface lightly dusted with icing sugar and cut out six cake shapes, following the template, to fit over the cookie. Spread the cookie with a little royal icing. Position, then press the sugarpaste onto the cookie to stick to the edges. Continue until you have covered the remaining cookies with all the pink, white, red and rose pink sugarpastes.

While the sugarpaste is still soft, mark on quilted effects with a knife and make swags with a crimping tool. Roll out the scraps of sugarpaste thinly and cut out small blossom flowers, hearts and thin ribbon strips to decorate.

Place the remaining royal icing in a paper icing bag fitted with a no 1 straight nozzle. Position the coloured blossom flowers and decorations onto the cookies and secure with a small blob of icing. Pipe on lines and dots and push the metallic balls into the centres of the flowers to decorate as shown.

Giftwrapped Celebration Cake

Serves 90

For the cake base:

1 x 13 cm/5 inch square Madeira
cake, covered in almond paste
(*see* pages 32 and 42)
1 x 18 cm/7 inch square chocolate
cake, covered in almond paste
(*see* pages 31 and 42)
1 x 25 cm/10 inch square rich fruit
cake, covered in almond paste
(*see* pages 28 and 42)

To decorate:

2.25 kg/5 lb ready-to-roll sugarpaste
blue paste food colouring
1 batch royal icing
icing sugar, for dusting
225 g/8 oz flower paste
cornflour, for dusting
ivory lustre powder

Reserve 225 g/8 oz of the white sugarpaste, then colour the remainder blue. Reserve one quarter of the royal icing and colour the rest blue. Knead 450 g/1 lb of the blue sugarpaste and roll out on a surface lightly dusted with icing sugar to a square large enough to cover the top and sides of the small cake. Use to cover the cake as per the instructions on page 68. Trim the edges, then place the cake on a thin, 15 cm/6 inch square board. Repeat with 700 g/1¹/2 lb sugarpaste for the medium cake, placing the cake on a thin, 20 cm/8 inch board, and 900 g/2 lb sugarpaste for the large cake, placing the cake on a 30 cm/12 inch square cake board.

Roll out the white sugarpaste thinly and cut into strips 5 cm/2 inches wide. Stick over the sides of each cake with a little cold boiled water to form a flat ribbon. Push four sticks of thin wooden or plastic dowelling, cut to the depth of the cake, into the base of the large and medium cakes. Stack the cakes on top of each other. Place the blue royal icing in a small paper icing bag fitted with a shell nozzle and pipe a border around the base of each cakes.

Roll out the flower paste thinly on a surface lightly dusted with cornflour and cut into 14 strips 5 cm/2 inches wide. Fold the strips over to make loops, pinch together and leave to dry on wooden spoon handles lined with clingfilm. Cut out four strips and cut 'V' shapes for the ribbon ends. When firm, brush the loops with ivory lustre powder and stick in position with the ribbon ends with the reserved white royal icing.

Calla Lilies Wedding Cake

Serves 80–100

For the cake base:

1 each 15 cm/6 inch, 20 cm/8 inch
and 25 cm/10 inch round rich
fruit cakes, covered in almond
paste (*see* pages 28 and 42)

To decorate:

2.25 kg/5 lb ready-to-roll
sugarpaste
pink, brown, yellow and green
paste food colourings
icing sugar, for dusting
1 batch royal icing
brown satin ribbon
450 g/1 lb flower paste
cornflour, for dusting

Divide the sugarpaste into 1 kg/2^1/$_4$ lb, 575 g/1^1/$_4$ lb and 450 g/1 lb batches. Colour the remaining sugarpaste pink, cover in clingfilm and reserve. Knead the largest batch until soft, then roll out on a surface lightly dusted with icing sugar to a circle large enough to cover the top and sides of the large cake. Cover the cake as per the instructions on page 68. Repeat, covering the medium and small cakes. Place the large cake on a 35 cm/14 inch round cake drum, the medium cake on a thin, 20 cm/8 inch round board and the small cake on a thin, 15 cm/6 inch cake board.

Colour three quarters of the royal icing brown and place in a piping bag fitted with a medium plain nozzle. Pipe a looped pattern interspersed with dots as shown, and leave to dry for 24 hours. Trim the base of each cake with the satin ribbon. Stack the cakes on top of each other using dowels as per the instructions on page 78.

Colour one quarter of the flower paste pale yellow, a quarter green and the rest deep pink. Following the instructions on page 71, make seven small, seven medium and seven large lilies. Leave to dry on nonstick baking parchment for 8 hours until firm. Roll out the green flower paste on a surface lightly dusted with cornflour and cut out three large, three medium and seven small leaves, mark on veins with a sharp knife, pinch the ends together and leave to dry for 8 hours until firm. Roll out the reserved pink sugarpaste to three strips, 14 cm x 26 cm/4^1/$_2$ inches x 10 inches long. Use a little white royal icing to attach the strips to the cake tiers as shown, pleating each piece at the top and base. Dab the lilies and leaves with a little royal icing and arrange on the cake, placing over the joins of the pink ribbon. Leave to dry for 4 hours until firm.

Daisy Birthday Cake

Serves 80–100

For the cake base:

1 each 15 cm/6 inch, 20 cm/8 inch
and 25 cm/10 inch round
Madeira cakes, covered
in almond paste
(*see* pages 32 and 42)

To decorate:

2.25 kg/4³/₄ lb ready-to-roll
sugarpaste
lemon paste food colouring
icing sugar, for dusting
1 batch royal icing
450 g/1 lb flower paste
cornflour, for dusting
white candles

Colour the sugarpaste pale lemon and divide into 1 kg/2¹/₄ lb, 700 g/1¹/₂ lb and 450 g/1 lb batches. Knead the largest batch until soft, then roll out on a surface lightly dusted with icing sugar to a circle large enough to cover the top and sides of the largest cake. Use to cover the cake as per the instructions on page 68. Repeat, covering the medium and small cakes.

Place the large cake on a 35 cm/14 inch round cake drum, the medium cake on a thin, 20 cm/8 inch round board and the small cake on a thin, 15 cm/6 inch cake board. Stack the cakes on top of each other using dowels as per the instructions on page 78.

Colour three quarters of the royal icing pale yellow and place in a piping bag fitted with a medium plain nozzle. Pipe a rope border around the base of each cake and leave to dry for 24 hours. Reserve the remaining icing.

Colour one third of the flower paste pale yellow for the flower centres. Roll out the white flower paste very thinly on a surface dusted with cornflour. Using a fine large daisy cutter, stamp out a daisy shape, then flute this up to flick out the petals. Roll a tiny ball of yellow paste, flatten out, then mark with a skewer to make the centre of the daisy. Press onto the middle of the petals and leave to dry for 24 hours on nonstick baking parchment. Make eight large, 16 medium and 30 small daisies. When firm, stick to the top and sides of the cakes with the remaining royal icing as shown. Press candles into the top of the cake to finish.

Floral Garland Birthday Cake

Serves 12–14

For the cake base:

1 x 20 cm/8 inch round Madeira
cake (*see* page 32)
4 tbsp lemon curd

To decorate:

1 batch royal icing
pink, green and yellow paste
food colourings
1¹/₂ batches vanilla buttercream
green and white ribbon trim

Make the piped flowers. Colour the royal icing in small batches of light and dark pink, light and dark green and yellow, and leave some plain white. Place a coloured batch in a small piping bag fitted with a flower petal piping nozzle. Place a small square of waxed paper on an icing nail and pipe a central dot. Pipe petals around this to make a rose. Pipe eight pink roses on squares of waxed paper and leave to dry for 24 hours. Pipe four white and four pink daisies onto squares and finish each with a yellow dot. Pipe 24 small, light green leaves, 12 dark green leaves and 12 white leaves onto waxed paper with a small, flat nozzle. Leave the flowers to dry for 24 hours, then peel away from the waxed papers.

Trim the top of the cake if it has peaked and cut the cake in half horizontally. Spread the lemon curd over one layer, then place the other layer back on top.

Place the cake on a 25 cm/10 inch cake board or flat plate. Colour the buttercream a light lime green with a few dots of paste food colouring. Spread the buttercream thickly over the top and sides of the cake, smoothing the top with an icing ruler.

Arrange the flowers around the outer edge of the cake, then place the leaves in between them. Attach the ribbon around the base of the cake to serve.

Topsy Turvy Flowers ❧ Stars Cake

Serves 80

For the cake base:

1 each 15 cm/6 inch, 20 cm/8 inch
and 25 cm/10 inch round
chocolate cakes
baked in topsy turvy cake pans, or
round cake tins, with one
sloping side trimmed away at
an angle, covered with almond
paste (*see* pages 31 and 42)

To decorate:

700 g/1¹/₂ lb flower paste
ivory paste food colouring
cornflour, for dusting
4 batches chocolate covering
icing (*see* page 56)
icing sugar, for dusting
¹/₂ batch royal icing
50 g/2 oz each large and small
white chocolate buttons
9 chocolate stars
floristry wires

Colour the flower paste ivory. Roll out thinly on a surface lightly dusted with cornflour and, using a three-petal cutter, cut out one set of large petals, five sets of medium petals and five sets of small petals. Curve the petals open and leave to dry in egg boxes lined with crumpled foil for 24 hours. Re-roll the trimmings into small balls for the centres.

Divide the chocolate covering into 1 kg/2¹/₄ lb, 700 g/1¹/₂ lb and 450 g/ 1 lb batches. Knead the largest batch until soft, then roll out on a surface lightly dusted with icing sugar to a circle large enough to cover the top and sides of the largest cake. Smooth down over the top and sides and flatten with an icing tool or your hands. Gather up the trimmings and repeat to cover the medium and small cakes. Cover the outer edges of a 35 cm/14 inch round cake drum and stand the large cake on this. Place the medium cake on a thin, 20 cm/8 inch round board and the small cake on a thin, 15 cm/6 inch cake board. Using dowelling as shown on page 78, stack the cakes on top of each other at angles as shown.

Colour half the royal icing ivory, place in a piping bag fitted with a no 3 plain nozzle, then pipe a rope border evenly around the base of each cake. Pipe a dab of icing onto the base of each button and press into the sides of the cake as shown. Stick the petal layers together with a little royal icing, stick on the centres and arrange as shown. Stick the chocolate stars onto the floristry wires, then arrange on top of the cake.

Children's
& Novelty

Children love colourful and creative cakes and treats – now you can satisfy their overactive imaginations with these wonderful projects. Featuring a charming array of sugarpaste critters, the Tropical Island Cake would make a great surprise for any animal lover. If you have a budding pilot in your midst then look no further than the Flying Pilot Cake, whilst the Ice Cream Sundae Cookies promise to taste as delicious as they look!

Spring Chickens Family

Serves 12–14

For the cake base:

1 x 20 cm/8 inch round lemon
Madeira cake (*see* page 32)

To decorate:

¼ batch lemon buttercream
1.3 kg/3 lb ready-to-roll sugarpaste
green, orange, yellow, blue, red
and purple paste food
colourings
icing sugar, for dusting
black food colouring pen

Trim the top of the cake flat if it has peaked and spread the buttercream over the top and sides. Colour 575 g/1¼ lb of the sugarpaste mint green, roll into a ball and roll out on a surface dusted with icing sugar. Use to cover the cake as per the instructions on page 68. Trim, then place on a 25 cm/10 inch cake board or flat plate.

Colour 225 g/8 oz sugarpaste orange, 125 g/4 oz yellow, 125 g/4 oz dark green, 75 g/3 oz blue, 75 g/3 oz red and 25 g/1 oz purple, leaving 50 g/ 2 oz white. Model two small chicks in yellow sugarpaste, then roll out and cut out eight yellow daffodil flowers with cutters. Model some orange sugarpaste into an oval shape for the mother chicken and stamp out six orange butterfly shapes. Mix a few mint green scraps with some orange paste and model the father chicken. Model beaks with orange and red sugarpaste and stick in place with a little cold boiled water.

Place balls of the dark green sugarpaste in an icing or garlic press and push out into long strands for the grass. Stick in small piles on top and around the sides with a little cold boiled water as shown. Roll out the white sugarpaste and stamp out 16 small white daisies; make yellow dots for the centres. Roll out the blue paste and stamp out 54 tiny blossom flowers. Roll out a scrap of red paste and stamp out 20 tiny red blossoms. Stick the daffodils, blossoms and daisies onto the cake as shown. Use the remaining scraps to decorate the feathers and beaks of the chickens. Paint dots on the faces for eyes with a black food colouring pen.

Princess Booties Cupcakes

Makes 12

For the cakes:

1 batch vanilla cupcakes
(*see* page 34)

To decorate:

¹/₂ batch vanilla buttercream
pink paste food colouring
500 g/1 lb 2 oz ready-to-roll
sugarpaste
icing sugar, for dusting
pink net ribbon

Colour the buttercream pink with a little paste food colouring. Trim the tops of the cakes if they have peaked, then spread the buttercream over them.

Colour 225 g/8 oz of the sugarpaste pale pink and divide into small balls. Place a ball in an icing press or garlic press and push out the sugarpaste until it comes out in strands. Place the strands in the pink buttercream to cover the top of the cake; repeat and cover all the cakes.

Leave 50 g/2 oz of the sugarpaste white and colour 225 g/8 oz deep pink. Roll out the white sugarpaste thinly on a surface lightly dusted with icing sugar and stamp out 24 small blossom flowers using a cutter.

Divide the pink sugarpaste into 24 small pieces and mould into tiny left and right shoes with a strap and button. Lightly dampen the daisies and stick onto the shoes. Place a pair of shoes on each cupcake in the pink topping. Tie a length of pink net ribbon around each cake, finishing with a bow.

Flying Pilot

Serves 12–14

For the cake base:

1 x 20 cm/8 inch round lemon
Madeira cake (*see* page 32)

To decorate:

¼ batch lemon buttercream
1.5 kg/3⅓ lb ready-to-roll
sugarpaste
blue, red, orange, black, brown
and pink paste food colourings
icing sugar, for dusting
blue trim
6 medium and 10 mini
marshmallows
1 mini Swiss roll

Trim the top of the cake flat if it has peaked and spread the buttercream over the top and sides. Colour 700 g/1½lb sugarpaste blue. Use to cover the cake as per the instructions on page 68. Trim, then place the cake on a 25 cm/10 inch cake board and cover the edges of the board with blue trimmings.

Roll out 275 g/10 oz white sugarpaste thinly. Cut out cloud shapes, dampen lightly with cold boiled water and press onto the top and sides. Roll out thin scraps and wrap around 10 small and 6 medium-size marshmallows, for the fluffy clouds, smoothing over the joins. Place on top of the cake.

Colour 225 g/8 oz of the sugarpaste red, 25 g/1 oz orange, 15 g/½ oz black, 15 g/½ oz brown and 50 g/2 oz for the skin. Roll out a little red paste, cut out the wings and fins of the plane and leave to dry on nonstick baking parchment for 2 hours. Make a small hollow in a mini Swiss roll, then roll out the remaining red paste to an oval large enough to cover it. Smooth over, keeping the joins underneath and place in the middle of the clouds. Model the pilot's head, body and arms with the skin-coloured sugarpaste and place the body in the cockpit. Roll out some orange sugarpaste thinly and make the jacket, propeller and wing trims. Stick on the jacket, make brown hair for the head and mark on the face. Secure the head onto the body with a toothpick. Roll, cut out and attach the finishing details, rest the wings on the clouds and attach the fins at the back.

Ice Cream Sundae Cookies

Makes 24

For the cookies:

1 batch butter-rich cookie dough
(*see* page 35)

To decorate:

1½ batches royal icing, made
from royal icing mix
blue, pink, brown, cream and red
paste food colourings
coloured sprinkles

Roll out the dough and cut round the templates on page 251. Carefully place on baking sheets and bake and cool as instructed on page 35.

Colour half the icing blue. Leave one third white. With the remaining icing, colour one quarter pink, one quarter brown, one quarter cream and one quarter red.

Place the blue icing in a small paper icing bag fitted with a no 2 plain nozzle. Pipe a thin line all around the outside of the sundae glasses, making a neat join, then leave to dry for 5 minutes. Thin down the remaining blue icing with a few drops water to make a pouring consistency, then flood inside the outline so that the icing covers the cookie. Leave to dry for 2 hours. Repeat the outlining and flooding separately with the cream, pink, brown, white and red icings, leaving each piece to dry before adding the next colour.

Finish the decorations. Pipe white lines around the sundae glasses and a border around the ice cream edges. Sprinkle coloured sprinkles onto the white icing on top to decorate.

Cook's Tip: To speed drying out of the royal icing, place the iced cookies on a baking tray and place in a very low oven set to 50°C/70°F/Gas Mark ½ for 15–30 minutes, carefully watching the trays.

Woolly Sheep Cupcakes

Makes 12

For the cakes:

1 batch chocolate cupcakes
(*see* page 34)

To decorate:

225 g/8 oz ready-to-roll
sugarpaste
pink, brown, cream and black
paste food colourings
1 batch vanilla buttercream
4 tbsp royal icing

Colour 25 g/1 oz of the sugarpaste pink and the rest brown. Roll the pink sugarpaste into 48 tiny balls. Divide the brown paste into 12 pieces and mould each one into an oval shape, then flatten out to make a head shape for each sheep. Pinch two top ends together to make ears. Dampen the pink balls and place four on each head to make eyes and noses.

Colour the buttercream pale cream with a little paste food colouring, then place in a piping bag fitted with a no 3 plain nozzle. Pipe the buttercream onto each cake in large blobs for the sheep's fleece.

Colour the royal icing black and place in a small paper icing bag fitted with a no 1 straight nozzle. Place a sheep's head on each cake and pipe black dots onto two pink balls for the eyes.

Rollercoaster Fun

Serves 20

For the cakes:

1 x 23 cm/9 inch square chocolate cake (*see* page 31)

To decorate:

575 g/1¼ lb flower paste
red, brown, turquoise, pink, yellow, blue, orange, green and black paste food colourings
cornflour, for dusting
½ batch vanilla buttercream
2.25 kg/5 lb sugarpaste
icing sugar, for dusting
¼ batch royal icing
silver balls
gold lustre paint

Colour three quarters of the flower paste red and one quarter dark brown, then roll out thinly on a surface lightly dusted with cornflour. Cut out four squares for the carriage fronts, 3 cm x 5 cm/1¼ inches x 2 inches, and leave to dry in a curved position over a rolling pin covered in clingfilm. Cut out eight side pieces, 5 cm x 2.5 cm/2 inches x 1 inch cutting out a curve on one side as shown. Cut out 4 x 5 cm/ 2 inch brown squares for the bases and four brown pieces, 3 cm x 2.5 cm/1¼ inches x 1 inch, for the carriage backs. Leave all the flat pieces to dry on nonstick baking parchment for 24 hours. Cut the cake as explained on page 244. Stick the pieces together with buttercream, then cut the wedge shape into two pieces. Stand the two pieces at right angles on a large board or tray, making a rollercoaster shape with two sloping ends as shown.

Colour 1.25 kg/2¾ lb sugarpaste turquoise, 450 g/1 lb light brown, 225 g/8 oz skin-coloured and 25 g/1 oz each yellow, blue, red, orange, green and black. Use the turquoise paste to cover the cake as per the instructions on page 68. Roll out the light brown paste into thin strips and use to make the track and side decorations. Place the royal icing in a small paper icing bag fitted with a no 1 straight nozzle. Pipe lines along the base and sides of the carriage pieces and stick together. Leave to dry on nonstick baking parchment for 4 hours until firm. Model heads, bodies, arms and legs from the skin-coloured sugarpaste. Decorate each body with a different coloured top. Place the legs in the carriages, stick on the bodies and secure the heads with toothpicks. Decorate with hair and paint on faces. Colour scraps of sugarpaste dark brown and make wheels, stick on and place a silver ball in each. Pipe lines on the carriage fronts with royal icing and paint over with gold lustre when dry.

Stars & Planets

Serves 90

For the cake base:

1 x 13 cm/5 inch square Madeira
cake, covered in almond paste
(*see* pages 32 and 42)
1 x 18 cm/7 inch square chocolate
cake, covered in almond paste
(*see* pages 31 and 42)
1 x 23 cm/9 inch square rich fruit
cake, covered in almond paste
(*see* pages 28 and 42)

To decorate:

3 kg/6 lb 8 oz ready-to-roll sugarpaste
royal blue, yellow, orange, green,
grey and black paste food
colourings
icing sugar, for dusting
225 g/8 oz flower paste
cornflour, for dusting
1 batch unbaked cake pop mixture
(*see* page 37)
thin lollipop sticks
ivory pearl and blue dusting powders

Colour 1.3 kg/3 lb of the sugarpaste royal blue, 575 g/1¼ lb yellow and leave 350 g/12 oz white. Roll out 225 g/8 oz of the yellow sugarpaste thinly on a surface lightly dusted with icing sugar and cut out 100 small stars. Roll the rest of the yellow paste into 80 large, 70 medium and 40 small balls. Leave to dry on sheets of nonstick baking parchment for 1 hour.

Use the blue sugarpaste to cover the cakes as per the instructions on page 68. Trim the edges, then place the cake on a thin, 15 cm/6 inch square board, the medium cake on a thin, 20 cm/8 inch board and the large cake on a 31 cm/12 inch thick silver board. Using dowelling as per the instructions on page 78, stack the cakes as shown. Dampen the underside of each yellow star and stick onto the sides of the cake. Stick the yellow balls around the base of each cake to make a border.

Colour half the flower paste a streaky blue and the rest in orange streaks. Roll both out on a surface lightly dusted with cornflour and cut out two large circles. Cut a centre from each circle and leave to dry flat on nonstick baking parchment for 24 hours. Roll the cake pop mixture into three large, four medium and three small balls. Colour the remaining sugarpaste blue, green, grey, orange, black and white and roll out into circles to cover the balls in various tones as shown. Stick the balls on thin lollipop sticks, dust with the dusting powders and place on the cake. Stick toothpicks into two large balls, then position the two large flower paste discs over the balls.

Psychedelic Giftwrapped Cake

Serves 20

For the cake base:

1 x 20 cm/8 inch square Medeira
cake (*see* page 32)
6 tbsp apricot glaze
(*see* page 42)

To decorate:

1.3 kg/3 lb ready-to-roll
sugarpaste
pink, lime green, yellow, purple
and blue paste food colourings
icing sugar, for dusting

Trim the top of the cake if it has peaked. Spread the glaze over the top and sides of the cake. Colour 700 g/1½ lb of the sugarpaste pink, then roll out on a surface lightly dusted with icing sugar to a square large enough to cover the top and sides of the cake. Lift the icing onto the cake and smooth down over the top and sides. Trim the edges neatly, then place on a 25 cm/10 inch cake board.

Colour half of the remaining sugarpaste green and the rest in batches of yellow, purple and blue. Roll out the sugarpastes thinly and, using shaped cutters, cut out yellow, blue and purple shapes to decorate the sides of the cake in layers as shown. Roll all the coloured scraps into small balls.

Roll out half the green sugarpaste and cut out four ribbon strips, 5 cm/2 inches wide and 25 cm/10 inches long. Stick the wide green ribbons on the four corners of the cake with a little cold boiled water. Stick the coloured balls around the base of the cake as shown.

Make the ribbon top. Roll out the remaining green sugarpaste and cut out 12 thin strips, 14 cm/5½ inches long and 2.5 cm/1 inch wide. Make each strip into a loop and pinch the ends together. Leave to dry on wooden spoon handles covered in clingfilm for 2 hours, or until firm. To finish, dampen the ends of the loops lightly with a little cold boiled water and stick onto the top of the cake in a tiered bow shape.

Fruit Cookies

Makes 20

For the cookies:

1 batch butter-rich cookie dough
(*see* page 35)

To decorate:

2 batches royal icing, made from
royal icing mix
red, green, orange, yellow and
black paste food colourings

Roll out the dough and, using cutters or using the templates on page 250, cut out four of each piece of fruit. Carefully place on baking sheets and bake as instructed on page 35. Cool on a wire rack.

Colour one quarter of the icing red, then colour the remainder in batches of light green, orange, yellow, dark green and black and leave a little white. Place the red icing in a small paper icing bag fitted with a no 2 plain nozzle and pipe a thin line all around the outside of the strawberries and the melon, making a neat join, then leave to dry for 5 minutes. Thin down the remaining red icing with a few drops water to make a pouring consistency, then flood inside the outline. Leave to dry for 2 hours.

Repeat the outlining and flooding separately with the yellow icing to make lemon slices and green for lime slices. Repeat for the round kiwi fruit shapes, flooding with green icing, then flooding the centres with white icing and using a toothpick to create a feathered effect.

Using dark green icing, mark on and flood the strawberry tops, then decorate the outer edges of the lime slices, melon and kiwi fruit with a dark green band. When the icing is completely dry, pipe white lines on the lemon and lime slices and white pips on the strawberries. Pipe black dots on the kiwi centres and on the melon slices for pips.

Cherry Cupcakes

Makes 12

For the cakes:

1 batch vanilla cupcakes
(*see* page 34)

To decorate:

900 g/2 lb ready-to-roll sugarpaste
brown, red and pink paste
food colourings
1 batch vanilla buttercream
icing sugar, for dusting
12 glacé cherries, washed
and dried
coloured sprinkles
floristry wires

Colour 125 g/4 oz of the sugarpaste brown and 125 g/4 oz red. Divide the remaining sugarpaste in half and colour half pink. Lightly coat the top of each cupcake with a little buttercream, then place the remainder in a piping bag fitted with a small star nozzle.

Roll out the white sugarpaste thinly on a surface lightly dusted with icing sugar. Using a round cutter, stamp out six circles 6 cm/2¹/₂ inches wide, then stick the discs onto the tops of the cakes. Repeat with the pink sugarpaste.

Roll out the brown sugarpaste thinly and cut into shapes to represent melted chocolate. Dampen the underside of the chocolate shapes lightly, then stick onto the cakes. Roll the red sugarpaste out thinly and roll each cherry in a small round of red icing to enclose it. Gather up the white scraps, roll out thinly and stick a small patch onto each cherry.

Pipe a small rosette of buttercream onto the top of each chocolate shape, then place a cherry onto this. Decorate with coloured sprinkles, then place a piece of floristry wire in the top of each cherry to finish. Remind your guests to remove the wire before eating the cakes.

Teddy Bears Family Cake

Serves 20

For the cake base:

1 x 20 cm/8 inch square Madeira
cake (*see* page 32)
6 tbsp apricot glaze
(*see* page 42)

To decorate:

1.3 kg/2 lb 10 oz ready-to-roll
sugarpaste
icing sugar, for dusting
grey, blue, yellow and black paste
food colourings

Trim the top of the cake if it has peaked. Spread the glaze over the top and sides of the cake.

Roll out 700 g/1¹/₂ lb of the sugarpaste on a surface lightly dusted with icing sugar to a square large enough to cover the top and sides of the cake. Lift the sugarpaste onto the cake and smooth down over the top and sides. Trim the edges neatly, then place on a 25 cm/10 inch cake board. Use white scraps to make a narrow strip to trim around the base, then press into position.

Colour 275 g/10 oz of the light grey, 125 g/4 oz blue and 125 g/4 oz yellow. Roll out the blue sugarpaste and cut out discs and half moon shapes, dampen lightly with a little cold boiled water, then stick onto the top and sides of the cake. Repeat with the yellow sugarpaste, cutting out shooting star shapes.

Make the bears. Roll two 50 g/2 oz grey balls for the bodies, then flatten one out to a teardrop shape and make one into a longer shape. Roll arms and legs and position as shown. Model a baby bear and place this underneath the father bear's arm. Roll two heads, then make tiny snouts and ears and press into place. Colour a little sugarpaste black and make into small dots for eyes and noses. Model a pillow and blanket for the mother bear. Stick the heads into position, securing with toothpicks. Place the pillow under the mother bear and place the blanket over her.

Fashion Accessories Cupcakes

Makes 12

For the cakes:

1 batch vanilla cupcakes
(*see* page 34)

To decorate:

1 batch cream cheese frosting
(*see* page 46)
pink and black paste
food colourings
350 g/12 oz ready-to-roll
sugarpaste
small silver balls
rose pink and silver lustre
powders

Trim the tops of the cakes flat if they have peaked slightly. Colour the cream cheese frosting pink, then place the frosting in a large piping bag fitted with a star nozzle.

Colour three quarters of the sugarpaste pink and the rest black. Model the pink sugarpaste into three handbags, mark with a quilting tool and press silver balls into them. Roll out thin strips of pink paste, then mark on ridges with a flat bladed knife. Fold over into three bows. Model the ends of three lipsticks. Leave all the pink items to dry on nonstick baking parchment for 2 hours, then brush with rose lustre powder using a dry paintbrush.

Using the black paste, model three pairs of shoes and decorate with silver balls. Model three black handles for the handbags and stick on with a little cold boiled water. Make three lipstick holders and stick on the pink end pieces. Brush the band around the lipstick holder with silver lustre powder. Leave the black items to dry as above.

Pipe the pink frosting onto the cakes in large swirls, then place the accessories in the icing as shown. Sprinkle over silver balls to finish.

Topsy Turvy Multicoloured Cake

For the cake base:

1 each 15 cm/6 inch and 25 cm/
10 inch round chocolate cakes
baked in topsy turvy cake tins, or
round cake tins, with
1 sloping side trimmed away at an
angle, covered in almond paste
(*see* pages 31 and 42)

To decorate:

2.5 kg/5 lb ready-to-roll sugarpaste
yellow, pink, purple, blue, green
and orange paste food
colourings
icing sugar, for dusting
floristry wires

Colour 1 kg/2¼ lb of the sugarpaste yellow and 700 g/1½ lb pink. Knead the yellow sugarpaste until soft, then roll out on a surface lightly dusted with icing sugar to a circle large enough to cover the top and sides of the 25 cm/10 inch cake. Smooth down over the top and sides and flatten with an icing tool or your hands. Gather up the trimmings. Repeat, covering the smaller cake with the pink sugarpaste. Place the large cake on a 35 cm/ 14 inch round cake drum. Place the small cake on a thin, 15 cm/6 inch cake board. Stack the cakes on top of each other at angles as shown.

Colour the remaining sugarpaste in 175 g/6 oz batches in purple, blue, green and orange. Roll the coloured sugarpastes and the pink and yellow scraps into 20 balls of each colour. Roll a small ball of pink sugarpaste and place in the centre of the top cake. Place a blue, pink, orange, yellow, green and purple ball onto pieces of curved floristry wire, then arrange on top of the cake, pressing the wires into the pink ball. Reserve the rest.

Roll out the remaining coloured sugarpastes and cut out small and large blossom flowers, large and small circles, strips and thin green sausage shapes and stick onto the cake as shown with a little cold boiled water. To finish, press the tiny balls around the base of each tier in alternating colours as shown.

Note: Remember to remove the wires before serving.

Cupcakes Cookies

Makes 24

For the cookies:

1 batch butter-rich cookie dough
(*see* page 35)

To decorate:

900 g/2 lb ready-to-roll sugarpaste
green, pink and blue paste
food colourings
icing sugar, for dusting
$^{1}/_{2}$ batch royal icing
small red coloured sweets
coloured sprinkles
small chocolate star sprinkles

Roll out the dough and cut into cupcake shapes with a cutter, or follow the template on page 250. Bake as instructed on page 35 and leave to cool.

Divide the sugarpaste into four portions. Colour one quarter green, one pink, one blue and leave the rest white.

Roll out the green sugarpaste on a surface lightly dusted with icing sugar and cut out eight cupcake base shapes, following the template, to fit over the cookie. Spread the cookie with a little royal icing. Position, then press the sugarpaste onto the cookie to stick to the edges. Continue until you have covered the remaining cookies with the green, blue and pink sugarpastes.

Roll out the white sugarpaste and cut out the tops of the cupcakes as above, following the template for the top piece, then stick into position over the coloured bases.

Place the remaining royal icing in a paper icing bag fitted with a no 1 straight nozzle and pipe on swirling lines to decorate as shown. Position red sweets in the top of the cookies and push into the icing. Scatter the centres with coloured sprinkles and chocolate stars to finish.

Resting Angel

Serves 16

For the cake base:

1 Madeira sponge cake baked in
a 2 litre/4 pint bowl
(*see* page 32)

To decorate:

50 g/2 oz flower paste
cornflour, for dusting
1.25 kg/2³/₄ lb ready-to-roll
sugarpaste
flesh, brown and pink paste
food colourings
¹/₂ batch vanilla buttercream
32 mini marshmallows
3 small yellow silver balls
2 tbsp royal icing
shimmer flakes

Roll out the white flower paste thinly on a surface lightly dusted with cornflour and cut out two wing shapes, then leave to dry on nonstick baking parchment for 24 hours.

Colour 175 g/6 oz of the sugarpaste a flesh colour and 25 g/1 oz brown. Trim the cake to a bell shape, then spread with buttercream. Spread the marshmallows with a little buttercream and stick together in four batches. Roll out four small circles of white sugarpaste and enclose the marsh-mallows. Gather the icing over them, leaving a lumpy surface, and place the join underneath. Place the marshmallow 'clouds' on a cake board.

Roll out the remaining white sugarpaste to a circle large enough to cover the bell shape and drape this over, smoothing over the top and loosely pleating the edges. Place the angel's body on 2 of the clouds.

Model arms, hands, legs and feet and a head from the flesh coloured sugarpaste and stick in position as shown with a little cold boiled water. Make a button nose and white discs for eyes. Mark on a mouth with a skewer, then paint the eyes with brown colouring. Secure the head to the body with a toothpick. Chop small pieces of brown sugarpaste for hair and stick in place on the head. Stamp out three small white blossom flowers and place a yellow ball in each, then place on the head. Spread the wings with royal icing, then dust with shimmer flakes and stick in place on the angel's back.

Busy Bees Cake Pops

Makes 12

For the cakes:

12 baked vanilla cake pops
(*see* page 37)

To decorate:

¹/₂ batch vanilla buttercream
700 g/1¹/₂ lb ready-to-roll
sugarpaste
black and yellow paste
food colourings
icing sugar, for dusting
12 thin lollipop sticks
block floristry foam in paper gift
container
2 tbsp royal icing
white chocolate buttons
silk green leaves and daisies

Coat each cake pop thickly in buttercream, then place on a baking tray.

Colour 75 g/3 oz of the sugarpaste black and the rest yellow. Divide the yellow sugarpaste into 12 pieces, then roll each piece into a ball. Using a small plastic rolling pin, roll one ball out on a surface lightly dusted with icing sugar to a circle large enough to cover the cake pop.

Drape the sugarpaste over the cake pop, trim and press the joins together until smooth, then roll between your palms to make a smooth finish. Repeat the covering and rolling process until all the cake pops are covered, then place them on lollipop sticks and place them in the floristry foam to keep them secure and upright.

Colour the royal icing yellow. Roll the black sugarpaste into very thin sausages then, wind three strips around each bee as shown. Cut the white chocolate buttons in half and dip each half in a little royal icing and stick either side of each bee as wings. Decorate the faces with very fine strips of black sugarpaste, then leave to dry in the floristry foam surrounded by silk green leaves and daisies before serving.

Tropical Island Cake

Serves 20

For the cake base:

1 x 23 cm/9 inch square Madeira
cake (*see* page 32)

To decorate:

¹/₂ batch vanilla buttercream
1.75 kg/3 lb 13 oz ready-to-roll
sugarpaste
beige, grey, blue, green, brown,
lilac, orange, yellow, red and
pink paste food colourings
icing sugar, for dusting
golden caster sugar

Cut one quarter out of one side of the cake and stick this to the back of the cake with a little buttercream. Cut around the sides of the cake to give it an irregular shape for the island. Spread the cake all over with buttercream and place on a large board or flat tray. Colour 700 g/1¹/₂ lb of the sugarpaste beige and roll out thinly on a surface lightly dusted with icing sugar to an irregular square large enough to cover the top and sides of the cake. Lift the sugarpaste onto the cake and smooth down over the top and sides, leaving the overhanging edges flat on the tray.

Colour 75 g/3 oz of the sugarpaste light grey, 125 g/4 oz blue, 125 g/ 4 oz light green, 175 g/6 oz dark green, 125 g/4 oz brown, 50 g/2 oz lilac, 75 g/3 oz orange, 75 g/3 oz yellow, 75 g/3 oz red and 15 g/¹/₂ oz pink. Roll the brown into sausages and press on for the palm tree trunks. Model a monkey with the remaining brown. Roll out the dark and light green sugarpastes and cut out leaves. Position the leaves on the palm trees and around the base of the island as shown. Roll out some blue sugarpaste for the sea and position as shown. Make sand castles with the orange paste. Sprinkle piles of golden caster sugar as shown and place the sandcastles in this.

Model all the animals with relevant colours and decorate each with faces as shown. Stick them in place with a little cold boiled water. Use scraps to make small flowers and stick these around the island to finish.

Candy Store Cake

Serves 40

For the cake base:

1 x 23 cm/9 inch and 1 x 15 cm/
6 inch Madeira cake, covered in
almond paste (*see* pages 32
and 42)

To decorate:

2 kg/4 lb ready-to-roll sugarpaste
ivory, red, blue, green and pink
paste food colourings
icing sugar, for dusting
glacé cherries, washed and dried
1/4 batch royal icing

Colour 450 g/1 lb of the sugarpaste ivory, 50 g/2 oz red, 50 g/2 oz blue, 50 g/2 oz green and 50 g/2 oz pink. Colour the remaining sugarpaste deep pink. Divide the deep pink sugarpaste into 700 g/1 1/2 lb and 450 g/ 1 lb. Use to cover the two cakes as per the instructions on page 68. Roll out the ivory sugarpaste thinly into two shaped rounds and cut out into shapes to represent drippy icing. Place the round over the pink icing on each cake and press into position. Roll deep pink sugarpaste scraps into a thin sausage and press around the base and middle joins. Place the smaller cake on a thin, 15 cm/6 inch round cake board. Stack the cakes using dowelling as per the instructions on page 78.

Roll out a little blue sugarpaste into thin sausages. Repeat with some pink, green and white. Roll a coloured strip together with a white one, then cut into short lengths to make candy twists. Make a square from light pink sugarpaste, roll scraps into flat ribbons, then pleat these and attach at each end of the square for sweet wrappers. Repeat with blue and green sugarpaste scraps. Make small balls from scraps of pink and red and place toothpicks in for lollipop handles. Roll scraps of pink and white icing and cut into large and small rounds. Stack the discs in the centre of the cake, placing the larger ones at the base. Wrap the cherries in thinly rolled red scraps. Place the cherries on the discs, making leaves from green scraps. Roll scraps of coloured sugarpaste into short lengths to represent coloured sprinkles. Arrange all the sweets on the cake as shown, sticking each with a little royal icing.

Templates for Sugarpaste Shapes

Roller Coaster Fun (not actual size)

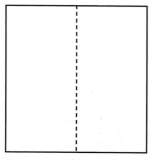

Cut cake in half as above. Cut one
piece into two triangular wedges.

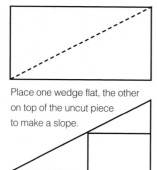

Place one wedge flat, the other
on top of the uncut piece
to make a slope.

Gingerbread House (not actual size – to be scaled up as per dimensions)

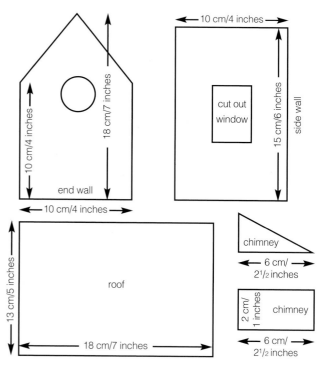

10 cm/4 inches

18 cm/7 inches

10 cm/4 inches

end wall

10 cm/4 inches

cut out
window

15 cm/6 inches

side wall

13 cm/5 inches

roof

18 cm/7 inches

chimney

6 cm/
2¹/₂ inches

2 cm/
1 inches

chimney

6 cm/
2¹/₂ inches

On these pages, you will find templates for some of the cake, cookie and icing shapes as used in this book. Templates such as these are handy if you do not have a selection of metal cutters. Just trace the pattern you want onto a sheet of clear greaseproof paper or nonstick baking parchment. Roll out the dough or sugarpaste thinly, then position the traced pattern over the dough or icing. Mark over the pattern with the tip of a small sharp knife or a pin. Remove the paper and cut out the marked-on pattern with a small sharp knife. Voilà!

Black & White Rose Cake

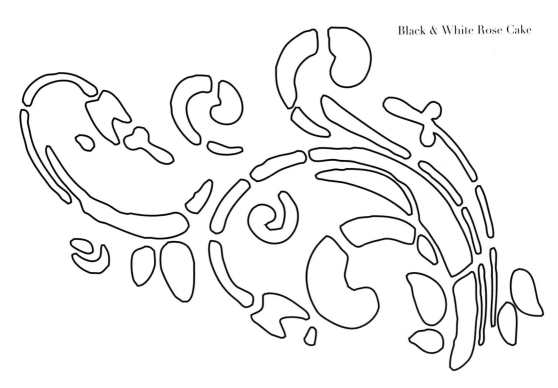

249

Templates for Sugarpaste Shapes

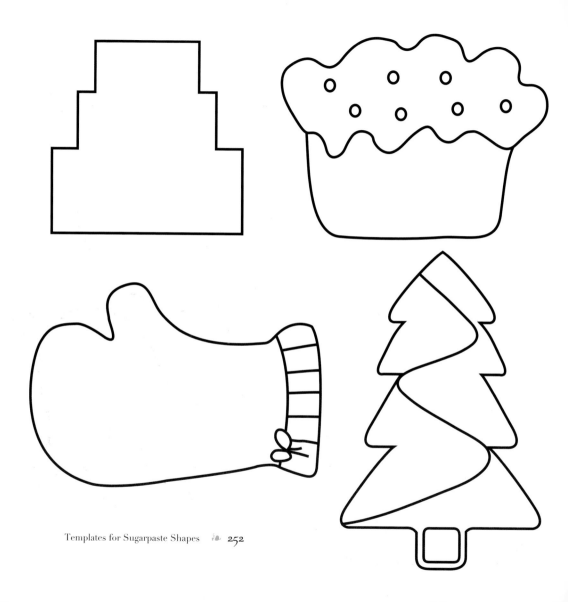

Templates for Sugarpaste Shapes

Index